The Mob in Hollywood

Adamo, Girolamo: AKA, Mo-Mo 4134 Lymer Drive in San Diageo. When, in 1955, Los Angeles Police Department arrested west coast hood Jack Dragna and his right hand man Girolamo "Mo-Mo" Adamo, they found a confidential address book that contained the addresses and names, and private telephone numbers, of some of the leading underworld mobsters in the Nation.

Adamo (left, and seated with (Left to right) Louis Dragna, "Tommy Blue" Dragna, Frank Dragna, Adamo and Frankie Paul Dragna

Among the names contained in this book was that of Tony Accardo, together with his residence address in River Forest, Ill. The book also contained the name of Joe Batters, which is the name frequently used by Accardo.

On August 4, 1967, according to police reports, Attorney Frank DeSimone (7838 Adoree Street Downey Calf.) became the boss of the Los Angeles Family following the death of Jack Dragna in February 1956.

DeSimone and LA-Chicago hood Johnny Roselli

Reportedly, in 1956 DeSimone raped Girolamo's wife, Marie, then 44, in front of Girolamo, who was 60 years old at the time. Several days later on June 18, Girolamo beat this wife in their rented beach house, struck in the head with an empty wine bottle, then shot her in the neck with a .32, and then committed suicide. The wife survived (She ran to a neighbor's house for safety and married hoodlum Frank Bompensiero.

DeSimone

Angelini Donald AKA The Wizard of Odds, Born 1926. Died December 8 2000 Correctly, Angelini was viewed by authorities as one of the top moneymakers in the syndicate history. He and Dominic Cortina reigned as gambling czars over a $20 million per-year sports betting empire. Angelini scoffed at the government's figures, but government agents insisted their numbers may even have been conservative. He did it by setting nearly unbeatable spreads on sporting events and controlled the odds for football, baseball, and hockey games.

Bill Kaplan, who had been around the gambling world since the days of Al Capone, was one of the last independent gamblers in the city in the 1960s. He had built up a lucrative racing and handicapping service on Clark Street that supplied odds to bookmakers all over the world in the years before the nation's scattered wire services were legislated out of existence by the government and supplanted by the Las Vegas casinos.

Alderisio

One day, "Milwaukee Phil" Alderisio's attempt to squeeze him out of business. It was just a matter of time before Alderisio grew tired of asking and simply killed Kaplan and Kaplan knew it. Kaplan went to mob lawyer George Bieber and Mike Brodkin and cut a deal, in which he would hand over 50% of his business in so long as the somber and deadly Alderisio stayed away from him and his business. It was a lucrative offer and the Outfit sent in the smooth, educated Don Angelini as the intermediary

Eventually, Angelini was selected as the Chicago family's replacement for Tony Spilotro out in Las Vegas, but by then, the mobs interest and influence had floundered.

Spilotro

Cops and crooks alike considered the refined and urbane Angelini to be a cut above the rest. Unlike the other representatives sent out to Las Vegas by the mob, Tony Spilotro, Marshal Caifano or Johnny Roselli, Angelina was a thinking man, a true gambler who never intimidated or killed anyone. Angelini, like Spilotro and Caifano, was barred from entering Las Vegas casinos by the state of Nevada and by the state of Illinois.

Splitting his time between Las Vegas, the West Coast and Chicago, in November of 1989, Dominic Cortina (Born 1929) and Angelini, pled guilty to charges that they ran a multimillion-dollar betting empire that took wagers on college and professional football, basketball and baseball games. (Others involved in the case included Joseph Rosengard, Joseph Spadavecchio Leonard Zullo, Raymond Tominello, Richard Catezone, Louis Parilli, and his brother, Charles Parilli) The group took in bets of up to $188,000 a day at 16 different locations in Chicago, Oak Park, and Bensenville Illinois.

Cortina organized the ring, supervised the booking offices, gave large bettors telephone numbers to place their bets, and paid out and collected winning and losing wagers from special gamblers, according to the charges. Angelini provided the point spread, known as "the line", and took bets from gamblers outside the Chicago area. In one instance, Angelini took bets totaling $16,000 from one out-of-state bettor on the outcome of football games being played by Boston College, Clemson, Nebraska, Mississippi, Texas and Southern California.

Auippa leaving court

Joey Auippa, greedy and thoughtless, demanded that Angelini and his boss Dom Cortina to explore all avenues outside of Las Vegas in an effort to determine new "skimming possibilities."

So Angelini found, eventually, the Rincon Indian reservation in California. In all likelihood, the Outfit would have passed on the Rincon reservation deal because it was such a disorganized mess, filled with tribal backbiting and politics. However, Angelini and DiFronzo came to the attention of the West Coast FBI after they made several messy collections out west. The Bureau taped their phones and gained information, most of it from the financier Richard Silberman who was involved with Angelini.

The plan was to finance the tribe's venture into gambling, take over the operations, skim money from the casinos as well as use it to launder money from narcotics sales. Dom Angelini placed Chris Petti, the outfit's man in San Diego, in charge of the takeover. Petti, in turn, was to deal directly with Angelini's brother-in-law, Michael Caracci, a soldier in the DiFronzo crew. The two hoods fought endlessly and complained about each other to Chicago through the back channels. Caracci contacted Petti at the same San Diego pay phone they had been using for years, which, unknown to them the FBI had tapped years before in a different case. The FBI sent in an undercover agent named Peter Carmassi, who presented himself as a money launderer for a Columbian drug cartel. The Chicago mob, in the meantime, had decided that Rincon was a bust and wouldn't put any money into it. However, they would allow Angelini and Petti to stay involved if they could find an outside source to finance the plan. Carmassi, the FBI agent, showed an interest. In several tape-recorded and filmed meetings with undercover agent Carmassi, Petti laid out the entire scam to take over the Rincon reservation gambling concession.

On January 9, 1992, the government indicted Petti, DiFronzo, Carlisi and the reservation's lawyer, on 15 counts of criminal conspiracy. DiFronzo and Angelini were convicted and got a 37-month sentence, with fines approaching one million dollars. Carlisi, DiFronzo and Angelini would all go to prison in 1993 on federal racketeering charges.

Carlisi was eventually released from the case but Angelini, DiFronzo were convicted, and each received 37 months for their part in the scheme. Both sentences were later reduced on appeal. Angelini died at age after fighting cancer for years. The Outfit never replaced Angelini out west and the position of Representato to Las Vegas is, by all accounts, no more.

Barzotinni, Dante: AKA Tino Barzie. Frank Sinatra Jr.'s manager. He purchased $50,000 worth of boasted airline tickets from gangster Henry Hill to fly Sinatra Jr. and a group of eight friends around the country. Barzie was caught and convicted.

Brooklier Dominic: Born Domenico Brucceleri. AKA Jimmy Regace. Born 1914 Died July 18, 1984.

Brooklier

Brooklier was boss of the LA mob in the mid-1970s. Brooklier came up through the ranks of the original Mickey Cohen gambling syndicate in southern California before defecting to rival Los Angeles mobster Jack Dragna's organization where he worked in pornography, extortion and burglary. By 1974, Brooklier was running the LA mob from prison through Jimmy "The Weasel" Fratianno.

When Brooklier was released from jail, he removed Fratianno. (Above) In turn, Fratianno implicated Brooklier for his involvement in the February 1977 murder of San Diego mobster Frank "The Bomp" Bompensiero and then entered the witness protection program. Amazingly, Brooklier was acquitted in the Bompensiero murder but was convicted in 1978 on federal racketeering and extortion charges and sentenced to five years imprisonment. He died in the Tucson Federal Prison in 1984.

Bompensiero Frank: Frank "the Bomp" Bompensiero was born in Milwaukee in 1905 and eventually made his way west to California. In 1937, Benjamin "Bugsy" Siegel, representing the national syndicate let it be known that West Coast gamblers would have to split their profits down the middle with him. One gambler who held out was Lew Brunemann, who had aspirations of controlling all the gambling in southern California.

Bompensiero

In July 1937, Bompensiero and one of his men found Brunemann strolling along Redondo Beach. The mobsters walked up behind him and put three slugs in his back, Brunemann lived. A while later, on October 25, Brunemann was having his dinners at the Roost Café, in Redondo Beach restaurant, with one of his nurses. Bompensiero and his gunman Leo "Lips" Moceri, a former member of Detroit's Purple Gang.

Bompensiero

Moceri said later "I've got a forty-five automatic and the place's packed with people. I walk right up to his table and start pumping lead. Believe me, that sonovabitch's going to be dead for sure this time. "Bomp's supposed to be by the door, watching my back to make sure nobody jumps me. I turn around and I see this football player ... coming at me. Bomp's nowhere in sight. Now I'm either going to clip this (guy) or he's going to knock me on my ass. So I blast him and run out, and there's Bomp already in the fucking car ... waiting for me. That guy showed me his color. If you ever work with Bomp, get him out in front of you instead of behind you." The police arrested the wrong man for the Brunemann murder.

On February 28, 1938, Moceri and Bompensiero kidnapped Phil Galuzo off a Los Angeles street. Bompensiero gave Galuzo a vicious beating and then shot him six times. After that, Bompensiero left the west coast and hid out in Tampa under the protection by the Trafficante Family. When he returned to Los Angeles in June 1941, the murder charges against him were dropped due to lack of evidence.

After Bugsy Siegel's murder in June of 1947, Los Angeles Mafia boss Jack Dragna attempted to take over the local gambling operations. Almost everyone fell into place except Mickey Cohen, one of Siegel's top men who were heavily into narcotics.

On Aug. 18, 1948, Jimmy Fratianno and his family visited Cohen's haberdashery shop to pick up tickets to the musical "Annie Get Your Gun". Outside a Mafia hit squad was waiting. Inside, Fratianno shook Cohen's hand and left. As soon as Fratianno was gone, Cohen, who had a clean fetish, retreated to a bathroom to wash his hands. Once outside, Fratianno signaled Frank DeSimone, Bompensiero, and three other men pulled up. Bompensiero, carry a shotgun, shot Cohen's bodyguard Hooky Rothman in the face.

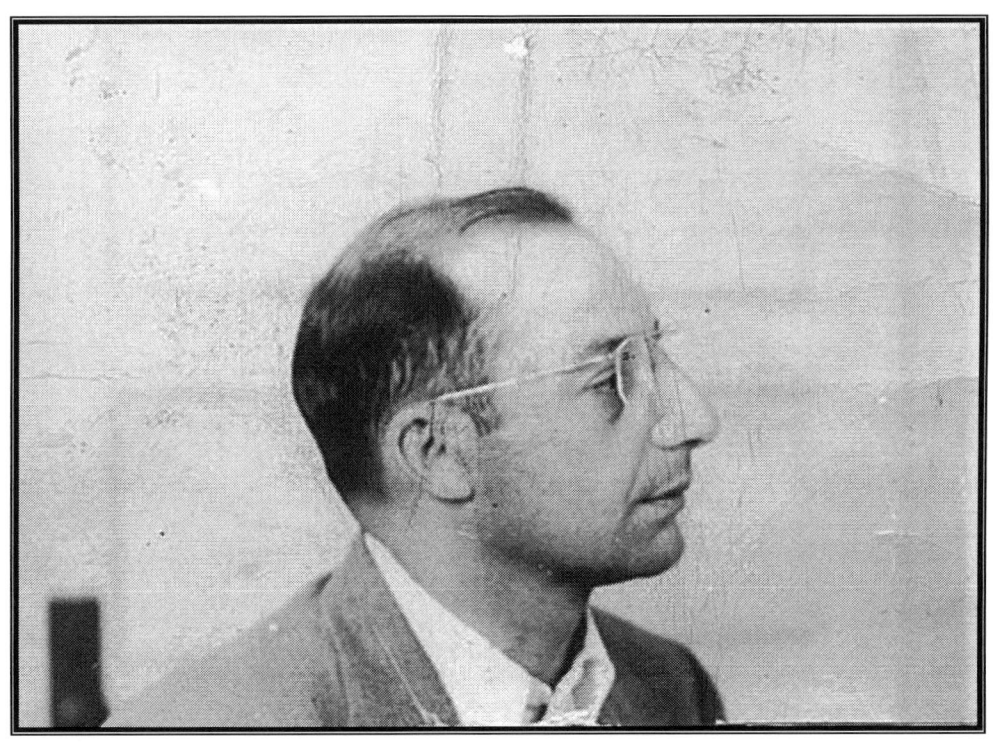

Frank DeSimone

Two other Cohen associates inside the store, Al Snyder and Jimmy Rist, were slightly wounded. Cohen escaped. Moceri later said, "It was Bomp's contract, and he blew it. Listen, (the others) didn't know Mickey from a lamppost, but Bomp did. They go in there and blast away at Al Snyder thinking he's Mickey. Then they shoot him in the arm, for Christ's sake. While this going on, Mickey's in the shitcan, standing on top of the sink. They didn't pump one slug through that door. Like a bunch of cowboys, they panicked and ran out instead of finishing the job."

In the very early 1950s, Jack Dragna appointed Bompensiero boss of the San Diego territory. Bompensiero kept office at nightclub they owned together, the Gold Rail. In the early 1950s, Fratianno met with Bompensiero to discuss plans to murder Frank Borgia, an ex-bootlegger still tied to Dragna. Gaspare Matranga was trying to extort money from Borgia who lodged a complaint with Dragna. Of course, Dragna was in on the shakedown, otherwise it never would have happened in the first place. When Borgia wouldn't pay, Dragna ordered Bompensiero to murder Borgia. Anthony Mirabile brought Borgia to Joe

Adamo's house. Once inside Mirabile grabbed Borgia while Bompensiero and Fratianno pulled a rope around Borgia's throat and pulled from opposite ends, choking him to death.

Fratianno

In 1955, Bompensiero was convicted on three counts of bribery and was sentenced to three-to-14 years in San Quentin. He served five. Fratianno was transferred San Quentin as well and Bompensiero made the mistake of telling him that he killed "Red" Sagunda, an ex-Cleveland thug who was operating in San Diego. In the meantime, Jack Dragna died in 1957 and was succeeded by lawyer-turned-mobster Frank DeSimone who drove the LA family into the ground. When he died in 1968, the group was taken over by Nick Licata, would prove to be even a weaker boss then DeSimone.

Licata

Bompensiero despised Johnny Roselli, the west coast representative of the Chicago mob in Los Angeles and Las Vegas, "These two guys (from Detroit) were having a feud and they went to see Joe Zerilli, each wanting the other guy clipped. So Mike Polizzi came to see me and this was strictly between us, nothing to do with the L. A. family. They tell me who they want clipped but I've got to do the job alone. As it happens I know the guy. So one night I see him at a party and I pull him aside. I says, 'Look here, you've been having this problem and the old man's given me the contract. I'm going to clip this guy but I'm going to need your help.' Now this guy's all happy, see, and I tell him I've got a bad back and I need him to dig the hole. We go out to this fucking place I've picked out ahead of time and this guy starts digging the fucking hole. Works like a sonovabitch, this guy, sweating bullets. So finally he says, 'How's that? Deep enough.' I'm sitting down, resting, so I get up and I says, 'It's perfect.' He starts climbing out of the hole and I shoot the cocksucker in the back of the fucking head. Back down he goes in the hole and I fill it in."

According to Bompensiero, he was supposed to receive a percentage of the profits from the Frontier Casino in Las Vegas as compensation for the hit. When Detroit reneged, Bompensiero went to see Johnny Roselli to make things right. Roselli ended up with a percentage of the casinos gift shop. Bompensiero never forgot the slight or forgave Roselli.

In 1967, Bompensiero became an informant for the FBI. In December of 1967 Johnny Roselli was charged with fleecing members of the Beverly Hills Friars Club out of $400,000 in rigged gin-rummy games. Seach, a member of the gang, who was granted immunity as a government witness if he testified against Roselli. Roselli learned about the deal and asked Fratianno to find Seach and kill him. He never did because Bompensiero notified the FBI and Seach was moved out to Hawaii.

In the early 1970s, Bompensiero did business with Anthony "Tony the Ant" Spilotro, the Chicago mob's new overseer in Las Vegas but otherwise continued to be a malcontent in the LA operation. When Nick Licata died in 1974, Dominic Brooklier took over the Los Angeles Mob and a year later, put out a contract on Bompensiero but Mob gunmen couldn't track him down. When Brooklier went to prison, Louis Tom Dragna, the nephew of Jack and the acting family boss announced that he was making Bompensiero Consigliere of the Los Angeles Mafia. It was little more than a trick to drag Bompensiero out into the open. They would wait to kill him.

Brooklier

The FBI learned that Fratianno was getting into the pornography business so the agency set up a dummy company called Forex and had Bompensiero tell Fratianno about the company. Several days later, Fratianno learned that Forex was an FBI sting operation.

Fratianno called Bompensiero and demanded to know where he had learned about Forex and why he wanted the outfit to get involved. Bompensiero lied and said that the information from a local pornography storeowner. When Fratianno told Bompensiero to bring the store owner to him, Bompensiero said that the owner had been killed several days before. They knew he was lying. On February 10, 1977, the 71-year old Bompensiero he was shot and killed by Thomas Ricciardi. Jimmy Fratianno eventually became an FBI informant and would later be forced into the Witness Protection Program. Suffering from Alzheimer's disease, died in his sleep at the age of 79 in June of 1993.

Borcia John Patrick AKA John Borcy. Born 1898. Arrested in Chicago's West side numerous times in the 1930s. He lived at 958 North Hamlin Avenue in Chicago. Borcia was a close friend of Tony Accardo's and Nick Circella. Primarily a jewel thief. In 1928, freelancers kidnapped his wife, Olive, as a means to extort $100,000 in stolen diamonds from Borcia. Borcia criminal record included one conviction in New York for murder in the late 1930s.

He operated the Primrose Path Bar at 1159 North Clark Street, in Chicago, which was probably owned by Accardo. In the late 1950s, he opened a second bar called the Primrose in Los Angeles, which had been owned by LA mob boss Jack Dragna.(1429 Thelborn West Covina and 4757 Kennsington Drive in San Diego. Dragna, by the way, died wearing pink pajamas) Police suspected that Dragna continued to run a brothel above the bar after Borcia took over. The bar was also known as a buglers meeting place.

Cohn, Harry: Studio owner. AKA King Cohn, a nickname he had given himself. Cohn rose out of the slums of New York, to become the head of a major American film studio. But, the streets never left him and Cohn was as rude, crude and vulgar. He regaled in his own ignorance and his ability to offend. As a producer, many people in the business considered Cohn to be the meanest, most vindictive and hard-nosed man in Hollywood, with a sadistic power fixation.

Harry Cohn

After visiting Italy in 1933 and befriending Mussolini, (he would keep a signed photo of the Dictator on his desk until the war started) Cohn returned to Hollywood and had his office remodeled after Il Duce's. His massive desk was raised on a dais from which he could look down at the writers and directors who worked under him; men like the talented Ben Hecht who despised Cohn and his famous temper tantrums, and gave him his nickname "White Fang."

Starlets who worked for Cohn had to endure at least one "hell week" of sleeping with Cohn if they intended to make it at Columbia, and, in 1948, it was Marilyn Monroe's turn. Cohn had always said that he considered Monroe "a second string no talent with tits" and that the only reason he hired her was that Tony Accardo, then boss of the Chicago mob, owned Monroe's career and had told Johnny Roselli to force Cohn into signing Monroe on with Columbia Studios.   Cohn had his way with Monroe of course, giving her bit parts in exchange for the favors, but one day when she was summoned to his office for sex, the fickle and moody actress simply refused to go. She told Cohn that she was madly in love with Frank Sinatra, a man Cohn never liked anyway. Word about Monroe's defiance got around the studios, and Cohn fired her. As for Sinatra, who was at the bottom of his career and probably had no idea what the erratic Monroe had told Cohn, he was blacklisted off the lot.

Sinatra

At about this same time, Cohn was producing the film "From Here to Eternity" and Sinatra, who had read the novel, desperately wanted to play the part of a character named Maggio, a slightly built but tough Italian-American. He was perfect for the part, and, if he got it, it would put him on top again . . . and Sinatra badly needed to get back on top again.

He was out of work, owed $109,000 in back taxes, his voice was gone, and his fans had left after he divorced his long-suffering wife and married the actress Ava Gardner. Sinatra, again without any knowledge of the rift that Monroe had caused between him and Cohn, met with Cohn on Columbia's lot and asked for the part of Maggio but Cohn refused. "Cohn looked at me," Sinatra said, "funny like, and said 'Look Frank, that's an actor's part, a stage actor's part. You're nothing but a hoofer.'" Nobody really knows what happened next.

According to Sinatra, who was already dogged in his career by the Dorsey story, Cohn changed his mind about giving Sinatra the part, after Frank agreed to take the role for $1,000 a week, a substantial drop from his usual price of $150,000 a film, even though nobody in Hollywood was willing to pay him a fraction of that price.

Dorsey and Sinatra

The other version of what happened was depicted in the film "The Godfather" when a decapitated $600,000 horse head ends up in the bed of a Hollywood producer named Jack Woltz. Woltz, according to the story line, refused to hire singer Johnny Fontiane, a Mafia don's godson, for a film "that will put me back on top again" and it does too, just as the role of Maggio landed Sinatra back on top.

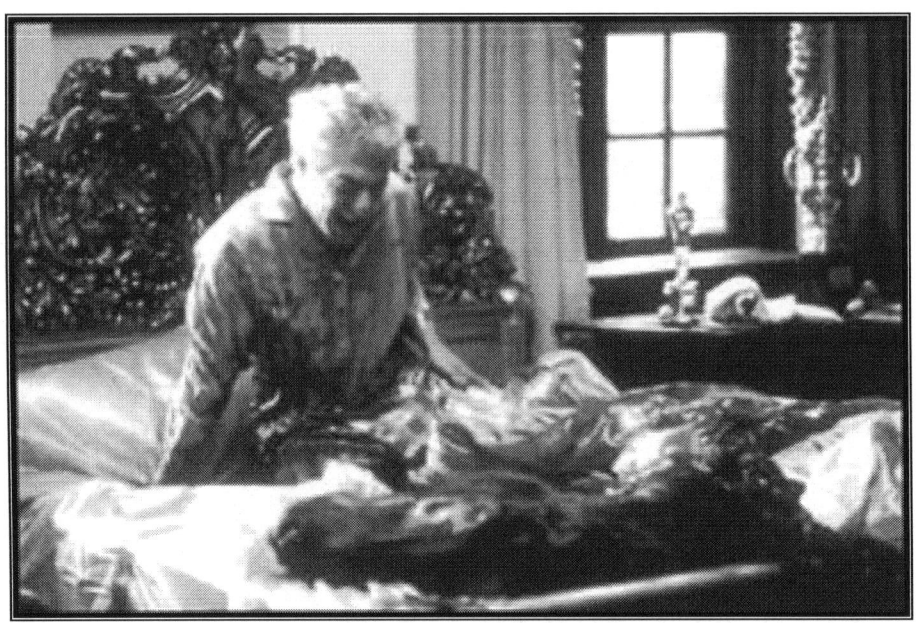

What is certain is that after Cohn turned Sinatra down for the part, that Sinatra called Frank Entratta, who fronted at the Sands Casino for the powerful New York Mafia Don, Frank Costello and his partners, labor goon Joe Adonis and Chicago's Paul Ricca and Tony Accardo.

Harry Cohn

Entratta was a close, personnel friend of Harry Cohn, they were regular fishing partners on weekends, but even the phone calls from Entratta didn't budge Cohn to hand the part to Sinatra. Then, according to Johnny Roselli, Entratta went directly to Frank Costello on Sinatra's behalf, and, working with Chicago's permission, Costello contacted Johnny Roselli out in Las Vegas and asked him to look into "this Cohn problem."

Johnny Roselli knew Cohn, they had first met back in the early 1930s right after both arrived in Hollywood and Roselli was still running numbers, and selling the occasional shipment of heroin around the studio lots. Cohn took an immediate liking to Roselli, which was easy to do, Roselli was chosen for the job by the bosses because he was likable. Soon Roselli was a regular visitor to Cohn's house.

On almost any weekend, the gangster could be found lounging around the pool or playing tennis on most weekends in the late 1930s and when Cohn separated from his first wife in 1936, Roselli found him a penthouse to live in at Sunset Plaza, a luxury bungalow complex at the opposite side of Columbia Studios, and Roselli rented the ground floor from Cohn.

Once, when Roselli remarked that he wanted to get out of the rackets and go into show business, Cohn offered him a position at Columbia as a producer at $500 a week, about four times the average national income. However, Roselli turned it down, saying "I get more than that from the waitresses who take bets from me."

The two men were so close that the FBI, who were tailing Roselli off and on over the years, figured he was Cohn's bodyguard. The core of the friendship was gambling. Cohn was a gambler and Roselli was his bookie, in fact Cohn was so obsessed with horseracing, he even had Roselli arrange to have a transmitter for the horse racing results brought directly into his office at the studio. He and Roselli shared a betting pool of over $15,000, an enormous amount of money in the Thirties, and Roselli, under orders from Chicago, made sure that Cohn got all the right information on which races were winners and which were losers.

Roselli also helped Cohn on the business front, like the time in 1932 when Cohn decided that he wanted to take control of Columbia Studios from his brother, Jack, who controlled the company finances from the corporate office in New York. The problem was that each brother owned a third of the company with the difference being held by a businessman named Joe Brandt, one of Jack Cohn's early partners. The Cohn brothers would meet occasionally in New York, but relations between them were strained, and toward the end neither would speak to the other without wittiness present.

The stress became too much for Joe Brandt, who said he would sell out to the first brother to give him $500,000 for his share of the business. Both brothers tried to raise the cash. However, it was in the midst of the Depression and the banks weren't lending, so Harry Cohn turned to Johnny Roselli for help. Roselli put Cohn in touch with New Jersey rackets boss Longy Zwillman, who was worth millions in cold, hard cash. Zwillman, who had deep interests in Hollywood, loaned Cohn the money to buy Brandt, no doubt taking his pound of flesh in return.

Cohn returned the favor to Roselli in 1937 when the hood had an opportunity to buy into the Santa Anita racetrack with Bugsy Siegel for $20,000. Cohn gave Roselli the money to make the deal and, several months later, when Roselli gave Cohn a check for the $20,000 he borrowed, plus interest, Cohn refused to take the interest money, and insisted that Roselli rewrite the check just for the balance owed. Roselli took the difference, and, reverting to an old Italian custom, purchased two matching rings, star rubies in gold, which would symbolize their friendship for life. Roselli wore one and gave the other to Cohn who wore it with pride.

When Roselli was locked away for his role in the Bioff scandal his name became poison in Hollywood. After his release from prison, Cohn, like so many other people in the business, didn't want anything to do with Johnny Roselli, in fact, when Roselli needed Cohn to put him on the payroll so he could get parole, Cohn refused, claiming that the studio's investors would balk. Roselli was stunned and hurt, and swore his revenge.

Now, using the Sinatra business as his excuse, Roselli would have his revenge. In a tense meeting in Cohn's office, Roselli reportedly ordered Cohn to give Sinatra the part of Angelo Maggio in the film. Cohn not only refused, he told Roselli, "John, if we have a problem here, I'm going to have to make some phone calls," referring to Cohn's own considerable contact in the underworld. But Roselli had the backing of the entire national syndicate behind him and knew that Cohn was defenseless. "Harry," he said, "If we have a problem here, you're a fucking dead man." In the end, Sinatra got the part and the Academy Award as well.

Cohen-Dragna War: Micky Cohen, born Cohen Meyer Harris Born September 4,1913 Brooklyn, New York. Died July 29 1976. Mickey Cohen was an affable, if slightly mentally unbalanced drug pusher in LA, by way of Chicago. Jack Dragna represented the local LA Mafia, the so-called Micky Mouse Mob.

Lou Rothkopf

Originally from Brooklyn, the Cohen's moved to Los Angeles in 1920, where Micky's father ran a drug store. At the start of prohibition, Cohen's older made gin in the back of the store at Micky, at age 9, was the operations delivery boy until he was arrested. Cohen turned to prize fighting in his teen years and had a brief but respectable career before he landed in Chicago and worked in the Capone organization at various odd jobs but was forced to leave town after he took part in a gun battle that left several gamblers dead.

Bugsy Siegel

Cleveland mobster Lou Rothkopf is said to have taken a liking to Cohen, something that was easy to do, and sent him to Los Angeles to work with Bugsy Siegel. When Siegel was murdered in 1947, Cohen was granted most of the dead gangsters gambling operations around Los Angeles. It was around this time that Cohen supposedly Cohen introduced a hoodlum named Johnny Stompanato to troubled movie starlet Lana Turner.

Johnny Stompanato

Stompanato and Turner

Stompanato dead

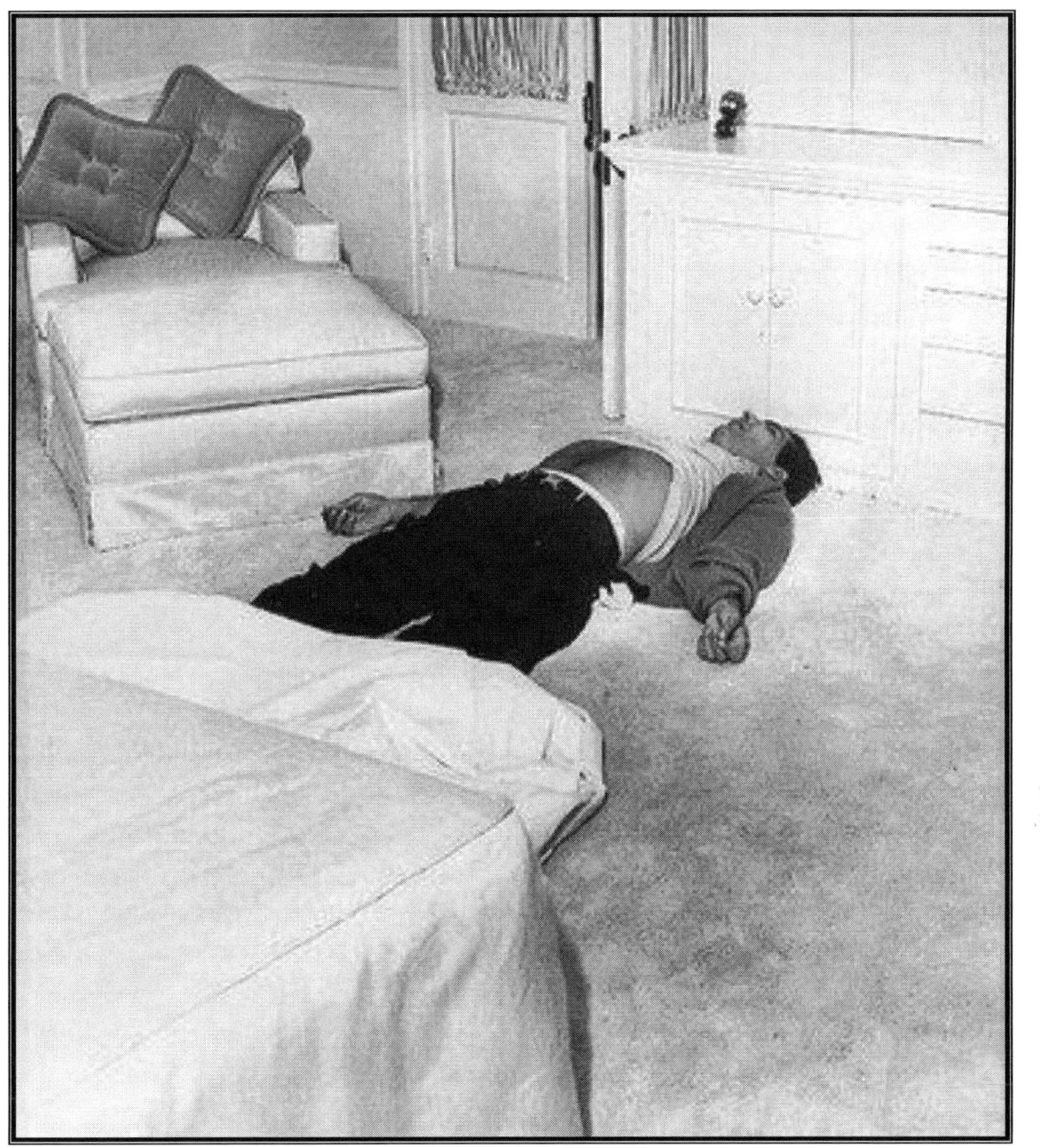

Cohen then wired Stompanato's bedroom and recorded the actress and Stompanato having sex and then pressed two thousand copies of the master recording and sold them $5 each. Turner's daughter, Cheryl, later stabbed

Stompanato to death in a killing ruled to be justifiable homicide.

Jack Dragna

The essence of the Dragna-Cohen war was control and power. Although Dragna was the unquestioned Mafia power west of Las Vegas, he felt slighted within the ranks of the traditional mob that moved in on Las Vegas without so much as a nod to him and generally disrespected by freelance hoods like Mickey Cohen and Jack Whalen who ran their bookie and narcotics operations. Dragna and Cohen could not be more different. Jack Dragna (He was born Ignazio Dragna but renamed himself years later in LA) was born on April 18, 1891, in Corleone, Sicily and arrived in the United States as a child. He returned to Sicily in 1908 and served a hitch in the Italian army. He then travelled back to the US in 1914.

Dragna is the suspected killer of Bernard Baff, a hapless kosher chicken wholesaler in Brooklyn. There is a possibility that Dragna worked with the New York mobs and the Capone operation at some point before venturing out west. Over the years, he had convictions for attempted extortion (1915) and served time in San Quinton prison. He was released in 1918 and never again arrested for a serious offense.

Dragna, who lived at 3927 Hubert Avenue in Los Angeles, took over the tiny LA outfit in 1931 after the boss, Joe Ardizonne vanished in 1931. (He lived at 10949 North Mount Gleason Avenue) A shy and retiring person, he avoided the limelight and the newspaper people. However, on April 15, 1951, when the LA police began a harassment campaign against the Mafia, the cops recorded Dragna having sex in his girlfriend's trailer at 330 Mariposa Street in LA and arrested him (and her) for engaging in lewd acts by consent (Oral sex)

Jack Dragna

Mickey Cohen, on the other hand, went out of his way to bring attention to himself, especially the press, which generally went lightly on him as a flashy, interesting character. Flashy, good humored and outgoing, Cohen quickly became the overall public favorite in the short lived, almost comical war with Dragna largely because Cohen understood the fundamentals of public relations. When an elderly widow named Elsie Phillips lost her house at 5631 Homeside Avenue in LA in a suit over an unpaid $8.00 radio repair bill, Cohen paid the lien judgment ($1,013.95) for her. Then his men beat the radio repairman up.

The shooting started when Dragna demanded a piece of the $40 per phone per week plus a general surcharge of $5.00 that Cohen was charging bookie. Cohen refused. So on Feburary 7, 1950, Dragna, planted a bomb under Cohen's home on 413 Moreno Blvd. in West Hollywood. (The same street where Jack Dragna lived)

The bomb, which went off at 4:15 AM, left a crater ten feet deep and broke every window in every house for 5,000 feet around. The explosion was felt seven miles away. The problem was, for Dragna anyway, was that his men had placed the bomb directly under a double laid cement floor where Cohen kept his safe. Because of that, the bomb blasted sideways instead of upwards. All that happened to Cohen was that the explosion lifted him up out of his bed and threw him back down again. His wife, LaVonne, their maid and the Cohen family dog were uninjured in the blast.

Cohen's car in front of Sherry's where the Dragna mob did a drive by shooting in an attempt to murder Cohen in July of 1949. It didn't happen. Cohen was slightly wounded, shot to the shoulder. His companion, journalist Florabel Muir, was hit in the rear end by a ricochet. Afterwards Cohen had his car bullet proofed and battle ready.

Members of the Sica gang were rounded up and questioned in the bombing but released when no evidence could be found to tie them to the case. "I am completely in the dark as to who done it" Cohen said and then added "And I ain't no gangster" The newspapers reported that Cohen was "almost put to tears" that his neighbors could have been hurt in the blast. One neighbor responded "That's very touching. What would be even more touching is if Cohen moved away from here" The neighbors then declared the Cohen "an intolerable nuisance" and demanded they leave the neighborhood. Cohen sent out a three- page letter to each resident, begging their forgiveness and asking that they reconsider.

Next, Dragna sent Sam Bruno to shot Cohen to death. Bruno was said to be the best shot in the mob. One bright, beautiful afternoon he hid behind a tree and fired a shotgun into Cohen's car as he drove by. He fired another round and effectively killed the car but Cohen was untouched. The bullets didn't even come near him. After that, mobster started saying, and probably believing, that Cohen made a pack with the devil. In Las Vegas, they were actually taking odds on how long it would take to kill him off and the odds were in Micky Cohen's favor. There were a number of failed attempts, all of which Cohen survived, basically through dumb luck.

The Kefauver Committee caused Cohen to be convicted of income tax evasion. He was sentenced to four years in federal prison. In 1961, a separate indictment found him guilty of income tax evasion in a second case. Sent to Alcatraz, Cohen was attacked by another inmate who hit the aging gangster in the skull with a lead pipe, dramatically affecting his motor skills."The guy" Cohen said "scrambled my brains" He was released from prison in 1972 and died in his sleep four years later.

Conrad Robert: (Born Konrad Robert Falkowski) The Chicago born film actor was a guest at the wedding of Tony Accardo's granddaughter, Alicia, when she married in a top rate ceremony at the Hilton Hotel in Chicago. Alicia once worked for Conrad in Hollywood. Conrad once said that the gangster Mikey Spilotro, Tony Spilotro's brother, was his friend.

Desimone, Frank: Tom Hagen, the Don's lawyer in the Hollywood The Godfather, was said to be based on Frank Desimone. A lawyer by training, he came to power after Jack Dragna. On June 18, 1956, right after he took over, his Underboss, Girolomo "Momo" Adamo, committed suicide in San Diego after seriously wounding his wife over an affair she was having with DeSimone. He was just as weak of a ruler then Dragna.

Licata

He didn't enforce things like he should of. He became a junior partner of the New York and Chicago Families. He was present at the Apalachin Conference. It was said that DeSimone lived in fear his whole life of being assassinated. He wasn't always wrong about that. Joe Bonanno actually did plan to have him killed when he planned to overthrow the other five families in New York. Joe thought he was a threat to him. He died in 1968 and was succeeded by Nicholas Licata.

DeSimone, Rosario: AKA Chief Born December 11, 1873- Died July 15 1946. Boss of Los Angeles, San Diego and Las Vegas from 1931 until his death in 1946.

He was the father of Frank DeSimone and a distant relative of Tommy DeSimone, (below) a real life character portrayed in the film Goodfellas.

Epstein, Joe: AKA Joey Ep. Born 1902. Lived at the Saint Claire Hotel, Chicago and 162 East Ohio Street, Chicago. An accountant/Book keeper for the Mob for many decades, his essential job was to launder cash for the Outfit. He was a business partner of Lenny Patrick of the so-called "Jewish arm" of the mob that once operated in the Rogers Park section. He was also romantically involved with Bugsy Siegel's girlfriend Virginia Hill and kept her supplied with cash for decades.

Hill, a foul-mouthed, tough-talking product of the poverty, had arrived in Chicago from rural Bessemer Alabama at age 17 in 1933 to work at the Century of Progress Exhibition. She tried a variety of jobs, waitressing, short order cook, (including a stint as a shimmy dancer for $20 a week, very good money at the time) but finally became a street walker. Hill was a beautiful young women and was soon taken in by the Fischetti brothers and more or less, adopted by Jake

Guzak and his bisexual wife, who offered to put her in charge of several brothels they still owned, but Virginia turned them down.

She said she had higher aspirations. The Fischetti's gave her a job as a waitress/prostitute at their casino, the Colony Club. Other owners in the club included Nick Circella (alias Nick Dean) who was later implicated in the million-dollar movie-extortion Bioff case. Circella's brother August Circella, ran the club.

August had run a series of casinos across Chicago including the Gold Coast Lounge, on North Rush Street. In later years, August would grow rich when he purchased the patent rights for a window unit air conditioner.

It was here that she met the bespectacled and withdrawn Joey Ep, a man who barely spoke to those around him. Nevertheless, he was dependable and honest, by mob standards, and had been Guzak's understudy since 1930 and would one day be his second-in-command.

Epp ran the outfit's racetracks with such authority the newspapers called him Illinois' unofficial racetrack commissioner. And while Epstein was well read, some said an intellectual, he loved to party and he was fascinated by the lowlife around him. He fell head over heels in love with Virginia Hill, and put her on the payroll as his mistress. But it was a working relationship as well. Epstein put Virginia to work as a courier, bringing suitcases full of the mob's dirty money

from Chicago, Kansas City, Cleveland and Los Angeles to syndicate owned and run banks in Cuba, Mexico, the Dominican Republic, France and Switzerland. There, the money was laundered, usually at a price of ten cents on a dollar and then invested in legitimate business from which the hoods could draw a salary.

The second part of the plan called for Virginia to get in touch with Bugsy Siegel, which she did, having met, and romanced him, several times in the past. Like Joey Epp before him, Bugsy Siegel fell head over heels in love with Virginia. He called her his "Flamingo" and drenched her in jewelry, furs and gowns.

When the Gangster Chronicles came on television in the late 1970's, a relative of

Bugsy Siegel remarked to Meyer Lansky, Siegel's lifelong business partner, that he was considering suing the production company for depicting Bugsy as an uncontrollable killer. "What are you going to sue them for?" asked Lansky. "In real life he was worse."

Unlike most hoods who dominated gangdom in the 1930's, Siegel (above) was smart and he knew it. He hated the poverty and ignorance of the world he was raised in and detested the illiterate and uncouth men he had to deal with. He wanted more, he wanted to be on the other side.

In fact, Siegel wanted to be on the other side, the legitimate side, so badly, that he invested a million dollars in the stock market in 1933, but lost half of it when the market crashed in October. "If I had kept that million," he said, "I'd have been out of the rackets right now." Siegel knew that if he stayed in New York, nothing would ever change, so he, and not the New York branch of the syndicate as is commonly reported, decided to try his luck out west in Los Angeles. He had been a regular visitor out there since 1933, introducing himself as an independent sportsman, a title that didn't fool anybody.

Of course, Bugsy had other motives. Gangsters always do. He had stabbed another hood in a dispute over a card game, cutting the man in the stomach 20 times to make sure gases would not allow his body to float to the surface, and now the cops wanted to talk to him about that. He had also been named in a scam to fix boxing matches and had ordered the killing of a bookie who had cheated him. When the bookie found out about the death order, he went to the cops and told them everything he knew, so for the time being it was best he went to the West Coast.

Siegel took over the Screen Extras Guild and the Los Angeles Teamsters, which he ran until his death. With control of the Screen Extras Guild, Siegel was able to shake down Warner Brothers Studios for $10,000, with a refusal to provide extras for any of their films. He also shook down his movie star friends for huge loans that he never paid back, and when he came back for another loan, he always got it, because they were, justifiably, terrified of him. He once bragged to Lansky that he had fleeced the Hollywood crowd out of more than $400,000 within six months of his arrival. He was a one man terrorist campaign.

When Siegel arrived in LA, the number one racing service out west was James Ragen's Continental Press, which serviced thousands of bookies between Chicago to Los Angeles, each of whom paid Ragen between $100 to $1200. The owner, Jimmy Ragen, was a tough, two fisted, Chicago born Irishman, who had punched, stabbed, and shot his way to the top of the heap, without the Mob's help.

The Chicago outfit, then under Nitti, watched the money flood into Regan's office with envy. Nitti, and later Paul Ricca, tried to set up a rival service called Trans-American, with each mob boss across the country running the local outlet, doing whatever they had to do to take Ragen out of business.

Frank Nitti

In California, Siegel and Mafiosi Jack Dragna were charged with putting Trans-America in business and taking Ragen's Continental Press out of business. Eventually, the Chicago mob settled the entire issue by shooting Ragen as he drove his car down a Chicago street. Ragen survived the shooting, but not the dose of mercury a nurse working for the outfit shot up into his vein a few days later. With Ragen dead, Continental Racing Services was divided up among the various bosses who had helped to build it, and Jack Dragna was named to run the California office. Siegel was shocked. He had risked his life to build the service out west, he had worked on it day and night, at the least he expected to be cut in on perhaps half the franchise.   Instead, all he was got was a visit from Chicago's chief fixer, Murray Humphreys, who told Siegel to fold up Trans-America wire service. They didn't need it anymore. The syndicate owned Continental Press. But Siegel sent Humphreys packing with a message for Paul Ricca… if the Chicago people wanted Siegel to fold up Trans-America in Nevada, Arizona and Southern California, it would cost them $2,000,000 in cash.

Virginia Hill, Bugsy Siegel's inspiration for the name of his Flamingo Hotel in Las Vegas (She had red hair) testifies before the Kefauver hearings. Primarily a money courier for the Chicago and New York Outfits, Hill refused to give the Committee any subtenant information. When one of the Senators insisted on knowing why mobsters bought her clothes, cars and houses she angrily replied "You want to know why? I'll tell you why…because I'm the best cocksucker in the United States, that's why. You got any more questions?" Her answer was struck from the record.

 Even though the Chicago outfit didn't want Siegel working for them, at the same time, they didn't want him working for New York either. Crazy or not, Siegel was smart, ambitious and ruthless. They had to watch him, so Paul Ricca told Charlie Fischetti, one of his most dependable torpedoes, to send out a spy, and the woman they chose was the same woman Bugsy Siegel came to call his Flamingo, Virginia Hill.

Charlie Fischetti with unknown woman

Virginia reported every conversation she had with Siegel back to the Fischetti brothers in Chicago. Still, the boys back in Chicago never trusted Hill, or anyone else for that matter, and when Paul Ricca came to power, he told Johnny Roselli to start an affair with Hill so he could keep tabs on her.

Paul Ricca

Then, Siegel watched a colorful Los Angeles hood named Tony Cornero move his entire gambling organization out of California and into Nevada where he and his brothers opened a rundown but very profitable casino on the Vegas Strip. Within a year, Siegel had the cash, most of it from the New York end of the syndicate, to build the fabulous Flamingo Hotel.

In May of 1947, one month before he was executed, Bugsy Siegel called Jimmy Fratianno, a Los Angeles hood who, technically anyway, worked for Chicago, and asked him to come out to Las Vegas for a meeting. He didn't tell them what it concerned, but, as they found out, it was a recruitment drive. He had already made the same pitch to Jack Dragna, Bugsy Siegel was planning the unheard of, and he was going to start his own organization out in the Nevada desert.

Virginia Hill had already reported Siegel's plans to Paul Ricca in Chicago, and, even though the Chicago mob was chiseling Siegel in the Flamingo by sending in professional gamblers to break the bank, they were indignant. As far as they were concerned, although the syndicate had agreed to allow Vegas and Reno to operate as open cities, it was clearly understood in the syndicate that Chicago controlled everything west of the Mississippi. Siegel was a regional problem at a time when the mob thought it had gotten over its regional misunderstandings. He was a relic from the past. He had to be removed.

On June 8, 1947, Virginia Hill got a call from Epstein back in Chicago, he told her to get out of town, to go to France, and she could tell Siegel she was going there to buy wine for the casino as she had in the past. He wouldn't question that. Virginia knew, immediately, why she had to leave town. They were going to kill Bugsy and the boys back in Chicago didn't want their best cash courier and narcotics peddler splattered with blood and headlines.

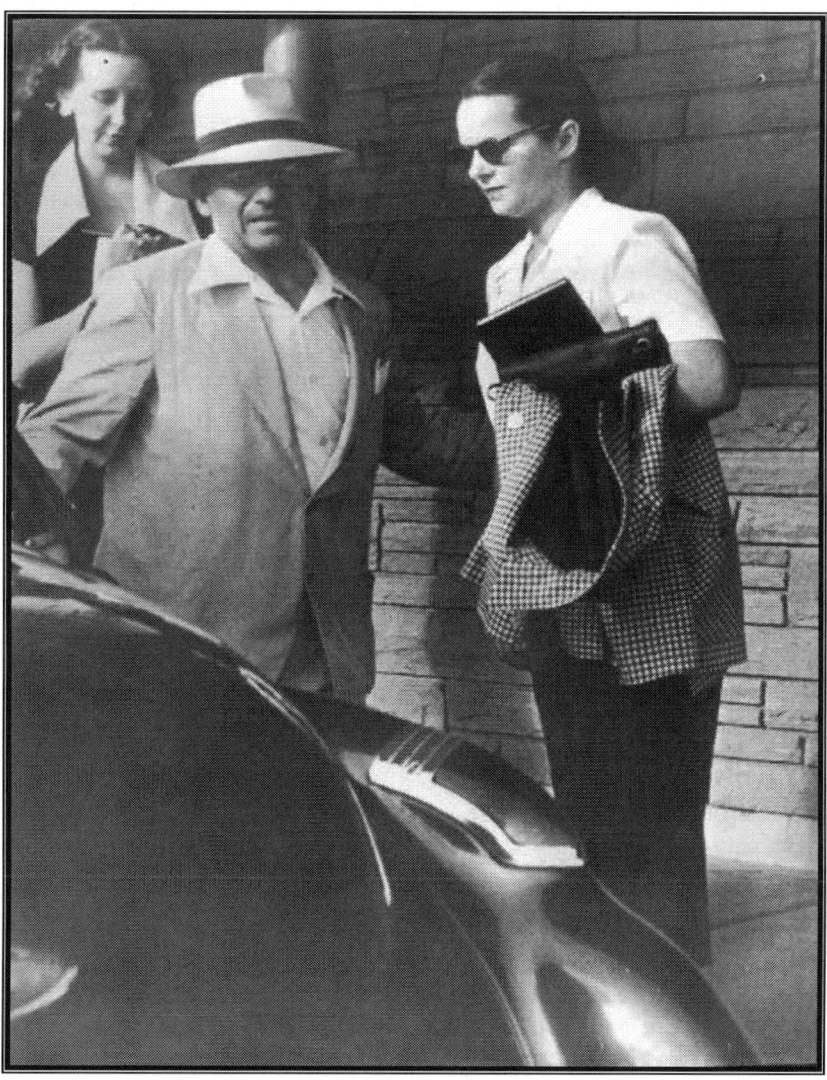

Virginia flew into Chicago and met Epstein at Midway airport, where he gave her $5,000 and then she continued to Paris. Back on the West Coast, Bugsy Siegel, caught in the middle of an uprising, was too busy to care where Virginia was. Several days before, Siegel told Micky Cohen to tell all of the bookies in Los Angeles, Reno and Vegas that the price for using the wire service was going to double. But, to Siegel's amazement, the bookies refused to pay, they knew that Chicago was taking over and that they were planning to kill Siegel.

And, on June 20, 1947, that's what they did. Jack Dragna gave the order to a hood named Frankie Carranzo. When the call came, Carranzo drove up to Beverly Hills and parked his car a few feet from Siegel's home, wound the silencer onto the barrel of his .30 caliber, army issue carbine, and walked around to the back of the house. He hid in the shadow of a rose-covered lattice work with his army carbine and released an entire clip into the living room through a 14-inch pane of glass. Nine slugs in all. Two of them tore apart Bugsy's face as he sat on a chintz-covered couch.

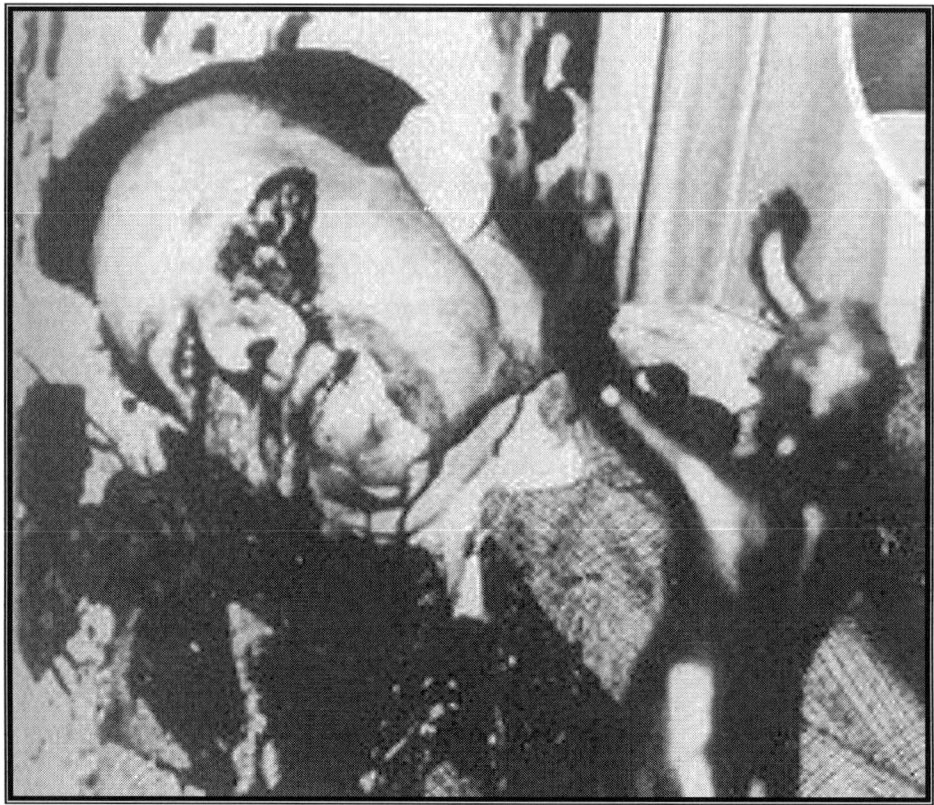

One bullet smashed the bridge of his nose and drove into his left eye. The eye was later found on the dining room floor, fifteen feet away from his dead body. The bullet was found in an English painting on the wall. The other entered his right cheek, passed through the back of his neck, and shattered a vertebra, ripped across the room. At exactly 11:00 A.M., Jack Dragna got a call from Carranzo: "The insect was killed," and he then hung up. A few minutes before that call, at 10:55, Little Moe Sedway and Gus Greenbaum, two hoods with gambling backgrounds, strode into the Flamingo and announced over the intercom system, "OK, we're taking over." Everyone present knew who "we" were.

The only persons to attend Siegel's funeral services at Beth Olam Cemetery were his brother and a Rabbi. Virginia Hill continued working for the Chicago outfit as a courier for several more years before they replaced her in 1950. She married a guy who wasn't involved with the outfit and had a child, but that ended in divorce. Joey Epp never fell out of love with her, and he kept her on the books for as long as they bosses would let him, but eventually even that stopped. In the 1950s when investigators followed a cash trail from Epstein to Hill, the gun moll was questioned about it by US Senator Charles Tobey who asked "But why would Joe Epstein give you money Miss Hill?" to which Hill replied "You really want to know?"

"Yes, I do" said Tobey

"The" replied Hill "I'll tell you why. Because I'm the best cocksucker in town"

When the cash did stop coming in, it was widely rumored in gangland that Virginia, desperate for cash, started to extort money out of Joe Adonis and other mob guys for whom she had carried narcotics over the years. On March 24, 1966, near a brook in Koppl Austria, a small town near Salzburg, two hikers found Virginia Hill's dead body. Austrian officials, not understanding who Hill had been, ruled her unusual death a suicide by poison. The Flamingo's next manager was Gus Greenbaum. He did his job. The hotel was completed and enlarged from 97 to two hundred rooms. By the end of the year the casino posted a $4 million profit, $15 million before the skim, clearing the way for the skimming to begin

Exner Judith Campbell: Mob mistress. Born Judith Katherine Inmoor January 11, 1934. Died September 25, 1999. Campbell was born to an upper middle class family in New York and settled in California while in her childhood. In 1952, she married actor Bill Campbell but divorced him in 1959. (The couple had been separated since 1955) Campbell claimed to have been working as an actress when Frank Sinatra introduced her to US Senator and Presidential hopeful John F. Kennedy on February 7, 1960 in Palm Springs California. She denied allegations and rumors from local law enforcement that prior to the Kennedy meeting she was working as a professional escort.

According to her statements before the 1975 U.S. Senate intelligence committee, Campbell said she had an 18-month affair with Kennedy before and after he entered the White House, and that she later had an affair with Sam Giancana while Giancana was boss of the Chicago Outfit. She also claimed to have been involved with Johnny Roselli, Giancana's man on the West Coast. In 1959 Campbell met singer Frank Sinatra, and they engaged in a brief affair.

A year later, on February 7, 1960, Sinatra introduced Campbell to Kennedy and shortly before that, to Sam Giancana. She swore under oath that there was no connection between Kennedy and Giancana, that her relationship with Kennedy was personal and not business and that she had no knowledge of any relationship between Giancana and Kennedy. Later, in her December 1975 press conference and again in her autobiography, she made the same denials and repeatedly accused the media of "wild-eyed speculation" for suggesting that she was an intermediary between Kennedy and Giancana.

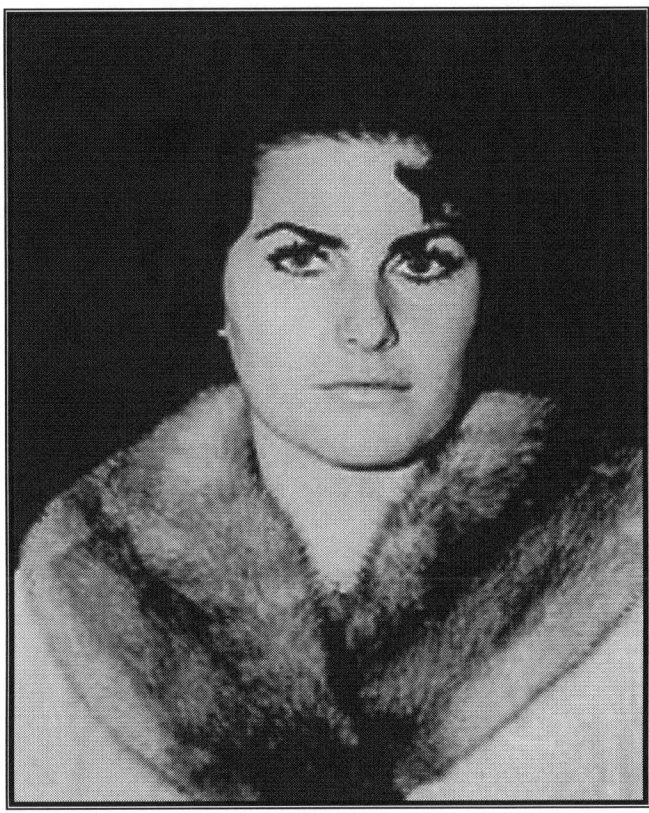

In 1997, 20 years after the publication of My Story, Campbell changed her story.

She unveiled new sensational allegations including a story that she was a conduit between the President of the United States and the Chicago Mob.

Campbell with her husband, Bill

She claimed that for 18 months, in 1960 and 1961, that she was the president's link with the Chicago Outfit and that she zipped across the country carrying envelopes between the president and Giancana, (concerning the Mafia-White-CIA plot to assassinate Cuban leader Fidel Castro.) and arranged about 10 meetings between the two, one of which, she thought, took place inside the White House.

Campbell, a long troubled woman with deep emotional instability, (Depression and paranoia) changed her story several times in a decade. It appears that virtually all of what Campbell wrote was concocted in order to sell a book and by the time she completed her autobiography in 1977, Kennedy, Giancana, and Roselli were safely dead. In 1988 People magazine interview Campbell said "I lied when I said I was not a conduit between President Kennedy and the Mafia. I lied when I said that President Kennedy was unaware of my friendships with mobsters. He knew everything about my dealings with Sam Giancana and Johnny Roselli because I was seeing them for him. I wouldn't have been seeing them otherwise."

Giancana

When pressed to explain why she had lied before the United States Senate she replied that she feared for her life if she told the truth "If I'd told the truth, I'd have been killed. I kept my secret out of fear." In fairness, it's not a completely groundless defense. Giancana was killed just before he was set to testify before the Senate committee and Roselli was kidnapped and killed right after he testified. However, it makes almost no sense for Kennedy to have chosen Campbell as his conduit to Giancana especially considering the vast numbers of more capable persons he could have chosen for the job including several mob-controlled US Congressmen.

What makes her claims so outrageous is that the wily Kennedy chose Campbell to act as her Mafia contact after having known her for less than two weeks. Conversely, she had known the paranoid Sam Giancana for less than a month before he supposedly agreed to accept White House messages from her. The strangest thing about Campbell's take is that Murray Humphreys, the Chicago Mob political contact and corruption expert, appears nowhere on the landscape.

Campbell said that her first assignment as courier was suggested by Kennedy at the dinner in his Georgetown townhouse on April 6, 1960. During the conversation Kennedy turned to her and said, "Could you quietly arrange a meeting with Sam [Giancana] for me?" Campbell said that the she called Giancana the next morning and arranged a meeting "I arrived at 8:30 a.m. on April 8th and talked to Sam at a Chicago club," said Exner. "I told Sam that Jack wanted to meet with him because he needed his help in the campaign." Giancana agreed, and the meeting was set four days later at the Fontainebleau Hotel in Miami Beach. "I called Jack to tell him, and then I flew to Miami because Kennedy wanted me to be there."

On April 12 Kennedy met with Giancana at the Fontainebleau. "I was not present," Exner said, "but Jack came to my suite afterward, and I asked him how the meeting had gone. He seemed very happy about it and thanked me for making the arrangements." Kennedy, a notorious skinflint, then paid Campbell $2,000 in cash. Writer Kitty Kelley, who assisted Campbell in writing her stories about Kenney and Giancana, speculated that the April 12 meeting concerned the West Virginia primary.

After Kennedy entered the White House, Campbell said, Kennedy continued to use her as a courier. A few days after the failed Bay of Pigs invasion in April 1961, Kennedy called her in California and asked her to fly to Las Vegas, pick up an envelope from Roselli and deliver it to Giancana in Chicago. Then she was to arrange a meeting between the President and the Mafia boss, one that took place in her suite at the Ambassador East on April 28, 1961.

Describing her role in arranging contacts between Kennedy and Giancana, she said "As a rule I would just call Sam. I learned to almost speak in a kind of code. I would usually say, `Have him call the girl from the West.' And if something was happening in Florida, it was, `Can you meet him in the South?' Sam always knew that `him' was Jack. I really became very adept. I think that I was having a little bit of fun with this also."

Giancana

Campbell claimed that FBI Director Hoover had agents tailing her so he could blackmail Kennedy with the evidence. However, according to Joe Pignatello, a Las Vegas restaurateur, mob insider and close personnel friend of Sam Giancana, the agents were assigned to follow Campbell only because of her involvement with Giancana and Sinatra and that agents had confirmed to Giancana Robert Kennedy had asked the Director to place a lock step on Campbell as part of his scheme to blackball Sinatra.

Pignatelo claimed that Campbell had worked as a paid escort on the Los Angeles-Las Vegas circuit and was hired by Sinatra to entertain Kennedy during their first meeting in Palm Springs on February 7, 1960 while Kennedy was a presidential candidate. It was Pignatelo's contention that Giancana had paid hush money to Campbell to protect Sinatra's career and not Kennedy's. "Sam" said Pignatelo "Wouldn't have pissed in the sink to help Kennedy. Why would help Kennedy with anything?"

According to Pignatelo, after the Kennedy's had cut themselves lose from Sinatra they attempted to distance themselves from him. According to Pignatello, the hush money used to bribe Campbell was taped to the inside casing of an old and no longer used oven in his restaurant in Vegas. Campbell died of breast cancer (some reports called it lung cancer) in 1999 at age 65.

The Hump in Hollywood: For almost four decades, Murray Humphreys was a major power behind the Chicago mob. A Welshman, the Hump started in the mob as an enforcer and labor goon for Al Capone. He seldom used foul or abusive language in proper company. Even Presidents Truman and Eisenhower, who knew the Hump, remarked that as hoods go, Murray Humphreys was a cultivated man.

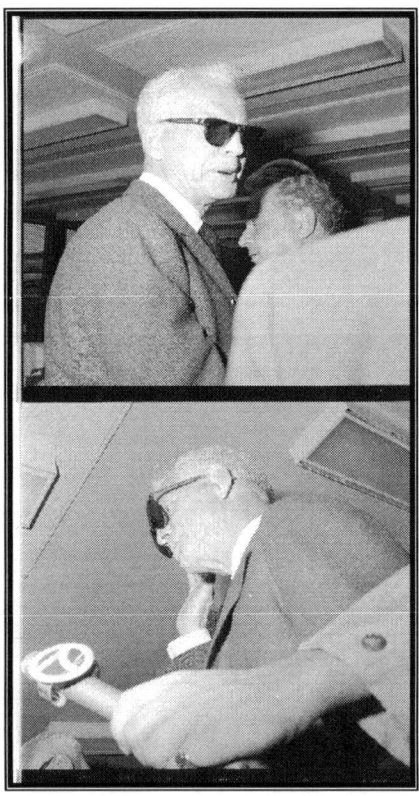

But, "The nicest guy in the mob," as Sam Giancana called him, this "Gentleman hood" was born with the disposition of a rattlesnake. Humphreys had blind ambition, brass balls, a love of money and a mean streak a mile long. He wasn't above threatening union workers with loss of a job or with taking out the eye of a dissident child or wife or mother. Murray Humphreys worked to educate himself not to be a gangster. He learned what to wear, when to wear it. He practiced his diction and improved his vocabulary. He was a dapper, short man who adored expensive and well-made suits.

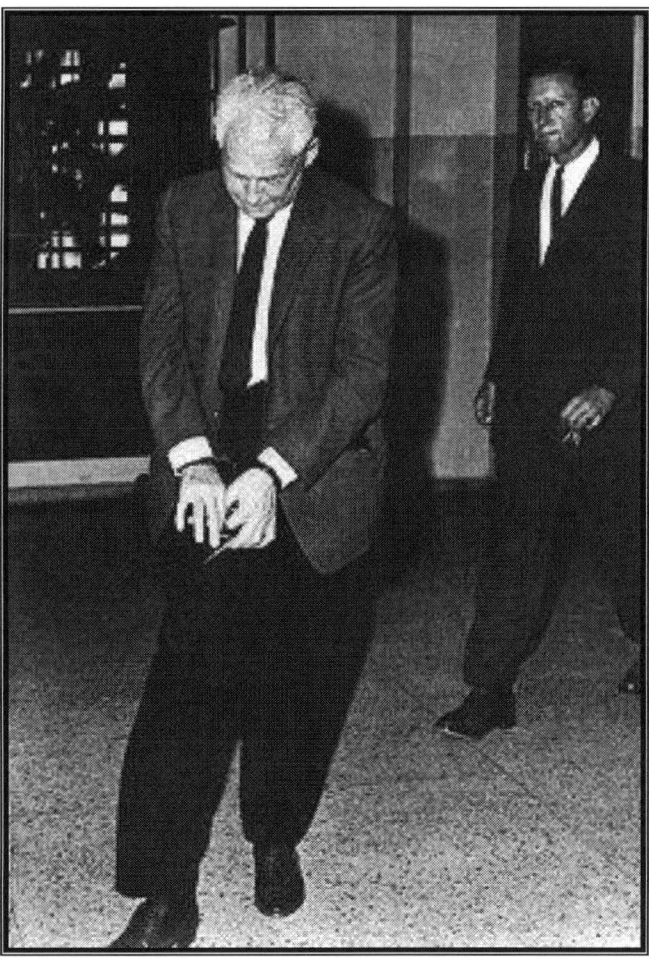

Humphreys, 1962

His elegant traits inspired a new generation of Chicago hoods who tried to mimic his style, the soft tone of voice, his slow, nasal diction which was void of any emotion when ordering a hit or a beating. In turn, Hollywood made hundreds of films based on smooth talking, cold as ice underworld characters that they watched flood into tinsel town from Chicago during the late thirties and early forties.

Humphreys was slicker, far smarter than most other hoods, and he skyrocketed through the ranks to become the outfit's chief political fixer.   When the Hump and his family visited Washington on vacation, Harry Truman personally showed them around Washington when he was the Vice President.

Humphreys daughter, Llewella, recalled that in the early fall of 1952 she walked into the living room of her house where her father was entertaining several men. The Hump asked her "What do you think of Eisenhower?" The teenager replied that she thought that he was fine man and that she would vote for him if she were old enough. At that very second, Dwight Eisenhower stood up out the easy chair he was sitting in and said, "Thank you very much young lady." (It should be noted that Llewella, who was widely loved by those who knew her, suffered from very series mental health issues)

Humphreys was doing time on a tax rap when the Bioff scandal went down, but a year after Bioff and the rest went to jail, the Hump was released and the family took a trip out west to Hollywood, where he met and befriended actor Fred MacMurray, whom he resembled. The two men remained lifelong friends.

 Humphreys had such a good time out in Hollywood, that Sam Giancana, then an up-and-coming star in the Chicago mob, took his own trip out west and arranged for studio mogul Jospeh Pasternak to squire his daughter around the studios and introduced her to Jimmy Stewart, Walter Pidgeon, Spencer Tracy and Greer Garson, while Giancana took care of business in Los Angles with Johnny Rosselli.

Llewella Humphreys recalled: "The outfit through the unions controlled every facet of the movie industry. And it all started with my mother, she was fan-crazy about movie stars. So she mentioned to my father, why don't we go into that business so I can meet everybody. So he, eventually, could make or break a studio by calling people out on strike. He loved making his own films, to editing, doing titles and putting on the sound track when sound came in. On holidays it was a nuisance with mother and myself twiddling our thumbs while he set up the camera. ...In those days the studios had tours as they have today, Joan Crawford was a very big star, at her peak then. She always worked on a closed set so that no one could come and see her. Mother really wanted to meet her. But this set on that particular day was especially closed because Joan Crawford had a scar on her face in the movie and didn't want anyone to see her. The head of the studio anyway, took mother an' me in. Joan Crawford stopped right in the middle of her scene and said, 'Get those two out of here. I will not have it on my set. It's closed.' The head of the studio went over to her and told her, 'Either they stay or you go, and you are through in pictures.' So we watched her make the movie."

Later, the family sailed off to Hawaii and returning by way of San Francisco, Humphrey's ship passed Alcatraz Island where Al Capone, Willie Bioff, George

Brown and a slew of other Chicago hoods were staying as guests of the government. Humphreys filmed the island and later added to the sound track, "The gang's all here."

Korshak Rodney Sidney: AKA The Fixer. In 1958 the McClellan committee wanted to talk with Gus Alex very badly and the committee told the FBI to find Gus Alex, subpoena him and drag him in for questioning. The problem was, the FBI had no idea where to find Gus Alex, who was lying low until the committee left town. The Chicago cops said they didn't know where Gus Alex lived. The FBI put Bill Roemer, the human bloodhound, on the case.

Korshak

What agent Roemer was able to find out was that in April of 1957, when Gus Alex and his wife applied for a rent at a posh Lake Shore Drive apartment house a letter of recommendation was written for him by state Senator R. Korshak, brother to mob lawyer Sidney Korshak. When Bill Roemer paid a visit to Senator Korshak to ask about the letter of reference, Korshak refused to cooperate denying that he even knew Alex "I only met the man once and that was on the street" and had no idea where Alex could be located. Next Roemer went to see Sidney Korshak himself at his Chicago law office at 134 La Salle Street. Korshak explained that he also barely knew Gus Alex, that their wives were friends. However Korshak did say that as far as he knew the Alex's were in Beverly Hills and Korshak had allowed them to use his white Lincoln Continental Mark 111 which he kept parked at the Beverly Hills Hotel.

Roemer also knew that Korshak had allowed the Alex's to use his villa at the Ocotillo Lodge in Palm Springs. Roemer said that he would be back to question Mrs. Korshak as to the where about of Gus Alex. Korshak blew up and told the hulking FBI man to stay away from his wife but Roemer stayed on Korshak.

One evening Roemer called Korshak again and Korshak surprised him by offering to set up an interview between Roemer and Mrs. Korshak in Beverly Hills that same evening. "I'll tell you" Korshak said "where you can reach her this evening. She will be at the Mocambo on Sunset Boulevard in Los Angles having dinner with Peter Lawford and his wife. I think you know who Mrs. Lawford is, don't you?" Roemer forwarded the information to Washington who elected to back off.

Sidney Roy Korshak began representing the Chicago Outfit in 1930, and acted as Willie Bioff's counsel during the Hollywood Studio scandal. Aside from representing the Outfits criminal and financial interests in Vegas and California, Korshak also ran a powerful law firm in Beverly Hills (Although he was never licensed to practice in California, he maintained no official Los Angeles office and had bills mailed from Chicago) and, due to his friendship with MCA founder Jules Stein and his chief aide Lew Wasserman, was a power within the Hollywood community.

When Korshak showed up unexpectedly at a Las Vegas hotel during a 1961 teamsters' meeting, he was immediately installed in the largest suite, even though the hotel had to dislodge the previous occupant: the union's president, Jimmy Hoffa. As an advisor and money manager, Korshak was so valuable to the Outfit lower-level hoods were ordered by their Skippers never to approach him.

Lormar Distributing Company: A company owned by Chuckie English (Tony Accardo and Sam Giancana were thought to have started the firm with their own cash) the company was a record sales and jukebox sales distribution firm that undersold competitors by selling bootleg copies of top recordings. On the hit record, You Can Make it if you Try; Lormar was thought to have sold 86,000 bogus copies to stores in three months. The pirating was flawless and even the color and coding from the recording companies label was perfect. In addition to buying records from Lormar, operators were forced to pay $3.60 per jukebox per year in protection money.

The messages to Midwest operators was simple, buy from Lormar or die, and most did. A rival wholesale record firm in one year lost $800,000, or 90% of its trade. The mob then decided to create its own singing sensation and introduced crooner Tommy Leonetti as their favorite and demanded that distributors fill their juke boxes with his records.

When one Chicago distributors named Ted Sipiora refused, saying: "It isn't good enough to get on the boxes." One of the hoods showed him a bullet and said "These things can be dangerous. They penetrate flesh." Soon afterward, said Sipiora, he began getting calls for the Leonetti record from operators who had heard the same sales pitch. When Sipiora told his story to the McClellan crime committee, NBC dropped Leonetti from its dance show American Bandstand. However, he was picked up by the Arthur Godfrey show, which wrongly assumed they were getting a trio called Tommy, Lee and Eddie.

Miller, John: Gangster Frank Costello was the godfather to John Miller, once an ABC reporter and FBI Assistant Director for the Office of Public Affairs, Miller's father and Costello were friends.

The origins of the Mob in Hollywood: The origins of the battle for Hollywood between New York and Chicago began in 1920 when Tommy Maloy, a union thug, took over the motion picture projectionist union local 110 in Chicago. Before the First World war Maloy had been a chauffeur to labor boss Mossy Enright but left just before Enright's murder in 1920. It was at that point that Maloy went into the movie business. Maloy didn't take it over exactly, it was called an inheritance.

Meaning that Maloy, as tough a customer as they come, inherited the right to terrorize the membership through the untimely death of another thug named Jack Miller who was killed when a bullet took out his right eyeball through the back of his head. Jack Miller had taken over the union from its first owner, a thug named Elmer Miller who made his collection rounds on a bike. It was Miller who formed the union by bringing in all the operators through threats of violence. Miller sold out his ownership in the union to Maloy so that he could open his own theater. At that point some hoods were trying to muscle in on the union; Maloy spread the story he beat up hoods who tried to climb into his booth where he was a projectionist. What really happened was that he was running a gambling game and they came to rob him. He really did beat them up and chase them out of the room at gunpoint. During the election, when he was spreading this story, a man named Williams ran against Maloy. Maloy's goons grabbed Williams, beat him and threw him out on the street and in five minutes he was elected business agent for the local 110.

Maloy carried the formal title of business agent, but he controlled hiring and legally collected monthly dues as the business agent, but for the most part Maloy ruled through blackjack and the Tommy gun and if a union member refused to pay dues he was replaced. Maloy had carte blanche to dip into the union till whenever he wanted. Maloy was also known for his skill as a blackjack, with brass knuckles.

He had no problems about cracking a man's skull, anyone who refused to sign up for his union, or of members who asked too many questions. Any projectionist who complained about the union books being closed to new members (yet having an empty till) was put out of work for ever if a theater refused to hire Maloy's members. He burned the film first, then beat the theater owner and finally burned the place down but in most cases he simply killed the theater owner and gave the place to a family member or gang crony to run.

Maloy was an ambitious little crook. Right after he took the projectionist union, he started working with Umbrella Mike Boyle of the electricians union. Their goal was to corner the entire building trades' business in the city, unfortunately for them they were both indicted for conspiracy by a grand jury in 1921 and charged with extorting money from builders to avoid labor troubles. Boyle refused to testify and the judge tossed him in jail for contempt but Boyle had been paying protection for years to the very corrupt Governor Len Small who granted him a pardon. In all, Small sold 8,000 pardons in the eight years that he was governor.

The Capone's never bothered with Maloy, who stood only five feet six inches and never carried a pistol, because he was a one man operation, and movies didn't become very big business until the later twenties, so it was assumed that Maloy was a small timer in a business that was interesting, but going nowhere. However, Maloy had alliances with the Capone, Moran and Saltis organizations, and other gangs. In order to keep them from taking over his union, he gave their men licenses and put them on payrolls to explain their incomes.

In one sense, Capone was correct, the movie business racket was small time, or at least it was until the advent of sound into film changed everything. As a result, movie theaters exploded in growth, yet membership didn't increase in Maloy's union, so he invented a scheme that called for theater owners to hire two of his men; one to run the film and one to synchronize the sound on the film. When Hollywood figured out a way to synchronize the sound with the film, Maloy agreed to let go of the second man in the booth for $1,100. That was less expensive than paying the projectionist on the payroll, so the owners agreed.

In his next ploy to raise cash, Maloy issued work permits to nonunion members and then closed the union to new membership. Regular union members had enough, and stormed the union hall in 1924, but Maloy's men defused the situation by firing machine-guns into the ceiling of the union hall. The members quickly took their seats and Maloy laid out his game plan for hiring non-union men as day workers with a permit.

Maloy explained that since the union members paid only $3.00 a month in dues, the permit workers would pay 10% of their pay check back to the union. This at a time when the average worker was making as little as $7 a week, Maloy's day workers were earning $175.00 a week, the 10% taken from them would be kicked back to the unions to help the membership buy more benefits and help those who were out of work.

The manufacturer's guide to projection machines bragged that "any intelligent young man can learn to run our machine in less than an hour" and went on to say that they were almost completely automated. Maloy made sure that they weren't and as a result theater owners in Chicago were years behind the rapidly advancing technology of the day and theater goers in the Windy City paid an average of 25% more for tickets than anywhere else in America.

There were problems, of course. In 1923 Maloy's office was at Harrison and Wabash where other labor skates like Con Shea of the teamsters and Steve Kelliher of the theater janitors had offices and together ran a gambling pallor on the first floor under their offices and shared the profits between the three of them. Maloy and Kelliher had a falling out over the proceeds of the gambling den. Maloy hired an up and coming O'Bannion goon named Danny McCarthy and invited Kelliher to join him and McCarthy for a drink at Tierneys resort on Calumet and 25th next to a theater where Maloy ran a theater. As soon as they were seated an argument began and McCarthy drew his gun and killer Kelliher. McCarthy pleaded self- defense and a dozen witnesses swore to it and he walked away from the murder rap Maloy took his union.

Just days before that, a hood named Big Tim Murphy decided that he wanted Maloy's union but when Kelliher was dead Murphy changed his mind. After Dan McCarthy shot labor leader Steve Kelliher dead at Maloy's behest, McCarthy took the plumbers union and sided with Dion O'Bannion and his boys. They shared the same lawyer, Michael Ahern, who also represented Roger Touhy. To close the deal, McCarthy took $150,000.00 from the plumber's union treasury and split it with O'Bannion and Weiss.

In 1927 Pete and Frank Gusenberg wanted their younger brother Henry placed on Maloy's payroll but he refused, sensing that the Gusenbergs might be trying to muscle in on his territory.

Frank and Peter Gusenberg

In retaliation, they ran Henry for president of the union against Maloy. The cops were called out in droves for the election, which was very violent. Four operators who came out for Maloy in the election had their car pulled over a curb and sprayed with machine-gun fire. Eventually a compromise was reached and Henry was placed on the payroll at $175 a week and he never had to appear at work.

A few months later, on August 29, 1927, the city's theater owners locked out Maloy's union. Across the city only seventy-five theaters, all small ones, were opened in the entire city. Jack Miller, the original owner of the projectionist union, led the revolt but not for idealistic reasons. He wanted to lead the owners and the projectionists as one. It didn't work, Maloy and his goons loaned out by Bugs Moran broke the lock out.

Maloy was rolling in cash, yet he was known to be one of the tightest hoods in the business. It was known that Maloy kept $100,000 in cash in a safe in his house. One time, independent kidnappers snatched Maloy's black housemaid and, by placing a pistol in her mouth in a car outside the house, convinced her to give them the keys to the house. But neighbors had witnessed the entire episode and called police.

Roger Touhy

Hearing the sirens approaching, the hoods took the key but released the maid unharmed. When some of Roger Touhy's boys kidnapped Maloy's bodyguard, Georgie Graham, they thought they had snatched Maloy. It was a humiliated Roger Touhy that had to call Maloy with the news: "Tommy, we got Georgie Graham, is he worth ten G's to you?" Maloy didn't pause a second, "Naw, he ain't worth a plug nickel to me." Touhy released the bodyguard unharmed.

Thomas J. Reynolds, Maloy's president, was on the payroll of Western Electric Company at $143.00 a week as a "consultant." He had been taken on by Western Electric in 1927, right after the company synchronized sound machines. It was that sort of blatant abuse that brought Maloy and his entire operation to the attention of the Internal Revenue Agency.

The IRS was out to get Maloy, and started by questioning Jack Miller about Maloy's income. When Miller refused to answer the question, Judge John P. Barnes locked him up for contempt of court. As instrumental as the I.R.S was in getting Maloy out of power, it was insurgents from inside the unions had provided the tax men with the information they needed to nab Maloy.

It wasn't the first time the membership had revolted. On two other occasions the rank and file stepped behind to insurgents who went up against Maloy and both times those men were found shot to death on the streets. Jacob Kaufman was a dedicated union organizer who had tried for years to have the courts get Tommy Maloy and his thugs tossed out of the unions. Maloy had warned Kaufman to back off but in June of 1931 Kaufman entered another suit against Maloy and announced that he would run against Maloy in an open election. Kaufman's candidacy meant trouble for Maloy since Kaufman had a reputation for honesty and was well liked by the rank and file.

On the night of June 20, 1931, Kaufman heard a can fall inside of his garage on Princeton Street. He told his wife to phone the police and walked from the house into the garage. When he opened the garage door somebody fired six shots into his head, killing him. Murray Humphreys was strongly suspected by police as being the killer for hire.

Another dissident who had caused problems for Maloy was 60-year-old Paul Oser who had brought Maloy to court several times in an effort to unseat him. In legal salaries, Tommy Maloy made $300 a month, O'Hara $150 a week for his services to the union. Oser had sent out anonymous letters to the members stating that Maloy had grafted $50,000 a year from the union. Oser's letter said that Maloy made $50,000 a year on the "permit men" as well. Oser had six children to feed but Maloy had denied him work for three years at a time when operators were making $90 to 150 a week.

When Oser went to New York to complain to the national union President, Fred Green, Emmert Quinn and his sluggers met Oser at the train station and beat him senseless in front of newspaper reporters and then Maloy fined each member in the party $5,000 each, to be paid at a rate of $5.00 a week. "Some of them," said Maloy, "got families. Just shows you I ain't all business." When Oser entered another suit against Maloy he and Maloy met in Judge John Patrick McGoority's chambers.

Oser thought that perhaps this was his moment of truth, the moment when the judge would force Maloy out of the union. But all Judge McGoority did was to encourage them "to met privately and work out their troubles like true gentlemen." After that, Maloy had enough of Oser and decided to kill him. He called in Thomas O'Hara to do the dirty work. O'Hara had been a dance hall operator before the First World War, then organized the piano tuners into a union and in 1919 became the business manager for the Chicago Federation of musicians but was tossed out for beating up the president of the national union. It was shortly after that O'Hara hooked up with Maloy.

Oser had been summoned to the office by Tommy Maloy for a peace conference although Maloy later denied that there was an appointment to see Oser and said that Oser simply showed up and said, "Let's work this out between us and to hell with them lawyers." They walked into to the inner office, Maloy said, when Oser suddenly drew a gun out of his pocket, forcing O'Hara to shoot him dead.

O'Hara said the same thing and Police did find a gun next to Oser's dead body, but it was not fired and it turned out that it belonged to O'Hara anyway. Maloy disappeared after the killing, hiding out at the Congress Hotel in a suite paid for by the union. Tubbo Gilbert, the State's Attorneys chief investigator, learned that Maloy was lying since he had interviewed Maloy's secretary, who said that her only words to Oser were: "Yes Mister Oser, you're at 2:30, please go right in."

But Gilbert may have had his own plan for the union as well. Right after the shooting, Gilbert seized all of the union's records, with orders to do so from his boss, the state's attorney. Those records ended up in Frank Nitti's possession, who took control of the union shortly afterwards. Remarkably, even in corrupt Chicago, a jury ruled that killing Oser was justifiable since there were no other witnesses to say otherwise. Judge Fardy agreed. Members of the jury were professional jurors selected under a political patronage system. After the trial, Coroner Frank J. Walsh issued an order forever banning the six jurors from ever serving on a jury again.

Tubbo Gilbert, "the world's richest cop"

On January 1, 1933, members of Maloy's unions lost a court battle to have Maloy and his thugs tossed out of the union by having the 1932 election results overturned and to have Maloy account for $230,000 in lost dues. The membership was shocked when the judge refused to grant a restraining order against Maloy, coming after the members who had sued because the membership had not proven Maloy to be a threat to them or anyone else. Then, on March 25, 1933, Ralph O'Hara, a 37-year-old "organizer" for Maloy, was shot and killed in his office by rebel fractions of the union in the afternoon as he sat in room 620 at 596 South Wabash Avenue. Maloy was losing his grip. He knew that if he wanted to retain control he would have to turn to the syndicate for help.

Frank Nitti had known Tommy Maloy for years. In 1934 Maloy called Nitti to ask for two favors. Maloy was a man of respect; he had nerve and he had guts, and he was tough, so Nitti listened. Maloy said the Treasury Department was all over him for a tax evasion case. They say he owed $81,000 in back taxes and it looked like he was going to jail. He needed Nitti to use the influence he had built up with the Treasury to have the case thrown off the books.

Frank Nitti

Secondly, Maloy said he wanted Nitti and the organization to back him for the presidency of the I.A.T.S.E. Nitti explained that he was already backing George Browne for the position, so Maloy asked for the Vice Presidency. He said that in exchange for the position, he would give Maloy a road map to I.A.T.S.E.

Maloy never figured that Nitti would double-cross him, but he did. Nitti told Maloy he would have to think it over and get back to him but actually Nitti figured that Maloy would get convicted on his tax evasion charges and the syndicate would waltz into the projections union and take it over. But, in November of 1934 it looked like Tommy Maloy would walk away from his tax case. It looked like he had worked out a deal by turning in Billy Skidmore, an independent gambler and bagman, over to the IRS in exchange for his own freedom. That was a problem for Nitti.

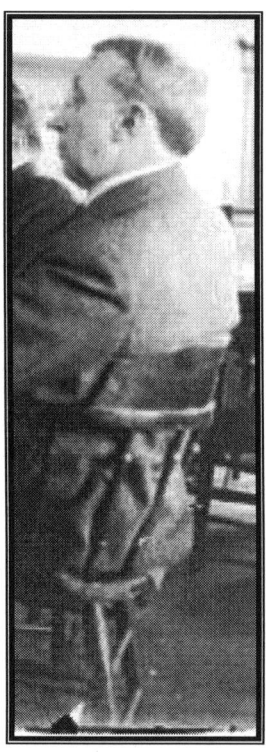

Billy Skidmore

If the syndicate was going to take over the movie industry they needed control of Maloy's union. But Maloy wouldn't give up his union without a fight, and the tiny Irishman was a force to be reckoned with.

On Christmas Eve, 1934, Nitti held a party for the outfit's top management and invited Browne and Bioff. During the evening the topic of Tommy Maloy came up. Nitti remarked that he needed control of Maloy's union to continue his domination of all the unions that ran the entertainment business. Anybody with ears knew what that meant. Nitti wanted Maloy's union for himself and Maloy was expendable. He was a dead man. They met again at Harry Hochstien's house in Riverside. Hochstien was a political leader from the 20th ward who owed his political rise to Frankie Rio. Also present at the dinner party was Charlie Fischetti, Frankie Rio, Frank Nitti and Paul Ricca.

Frankie Rio

They had drinks and then plates of hot food served from chafing dishes, followed by Italian espresso coffee and a wedge of spumoni ice cream. After the meal, and puffing on gigantic Cuban cigars, Nitti mentioned Tommy Maloy's union and said that they should take it over as soon as possible. Bioff reported later that there was a silence at the table. They all knew Maloy and liked him. According to Bioff, Frankie Rio turned to Nitti and said "Will Maloy stand for partners moving in on him?" Nitti said "Not Maloy."

Ricca said, "Can we scare him?"

Nitti answered "not at all."

There was another long pause and Nitti broke it and said, "We really ought to have the projectionists." Rio said, "I'll take care of it right after the first of the year."

Paul Ricca

Two months later on February 4, 1935, a bitter cold, icy Chicago morning, Maloy was speeding down the street with Doc Quinlan, a dentist and renowned union racketeer. They were on their way to visit Maloy's mistress that he had been keeping for the past two years, a beautiful chorus girl. As they pulled Maloy's Cadillac in front of the deserted building that was to house the century of progress exhibition, a car pulled alongside Maloy's Cadillac on Lake Shore Drive and fired machine guns into Maloy's body.

They fired enough shots to almost take off the entire left-hand side of Maloy's face. What was left of him was slumped over the steering wheel of his car which had smashed into a fire hydrant. He was 42 years old. George Browne was a pallbearer at Maloy's funnel. Two thousand people, curious onlookers mostly, lined the frozen streets to watch the hood get buried. The Mob was on its way to Hollywood.

Bioff Willie His name is barely known today, but for almost a decade he was at the forefront of what remains the largest extortion case in the history of American criminal justice, that set the foundation of modern organized crime. When the national depression knocked the bottom out of Chicago's once enormous prostitution racket, Bioff, a pimp, started to shake down Fulton Street shopkeepers, restricting himself to the Jewish stores and thus allowing George Brown, another goon whom Bioff knew only in passing, to work the Gentile side of the street. Since Brown and Bioff collected their payoffs from Fulton Street at the same time of the day, on the same day of the week, they starting talking and soon formed a partnership dubbed B&B, for Brown and Bioff.

Together, Brown and Bioff merged their shake down operations on Fulton Street and expanded their control of the stagehand's union by increasing dues by $5.00, and then pocketing the increase for themselves. Since that plan worked out so easily, over dinner one night they came up with another plan to raise more money, by threatening the theaters with a strike. Bioff came up with an even better idea. Instead of collecting money once from the theater owners, they would sell them a "a no strike guarantee," which they would collect monthly. The two hoods approached Barney Balaban, owner of Chicago's largest and most successful movie house chain, Balaban and Katz theaters. Sam Katz, who would go on to own MGM Studios, and Barney Balaban, who would one day run Paramount, had begun operating nickelodeons as teenagers, and in 1916, were among the very first to produce silent films. Balaban was a tough, two fisted, self-made man and when Bioff and Brown showed up with their extortion threats, he personally threw them out of the building, no small chore.

Bioff and Brown talked about it and decided that they entered into the shakedown the wrong way because they were unsure of themselves and nervous, and it showed. A few days later, they went back, more self-assured, and promised Balaban that if they didn't get their way, there would be a strike, it would last for months . . . unless Balaban gave $20,000 to B&B Enterprises.

To soften the blow, Bioff told Balaban that the money was to go directly to unemployed union members, for emergency help, like a soup kitchen. It was a lie of course. They intended, in fact they did, steal every penny of the money. But Bioff was smart enough to know that if Balaban gave the $20,000 to a charitable cause, like a soup kitchen, then the company could write the money off of their corporate tax bill and win public admiration at the same time.

Barney Balaban was also a shrewd dealer. He quickly figured out that neither Bioff nor Brown would keep any written documents of the transaction since they intended to steal the money anyway. That meant that Balaban and Katz could fork over $20,000 to Bioff and Brown's "soup kitchen" and tell the government they had donated $100,000 and then pocket the additional $80,000 for themselves. The beauty of it was, Bioff and Brown would swear that they had been given any amount Balaban said they had been given. They had to. They had no other choice. Brown and Bioff got the twenty grand. In cash. It was delivered by Balaban's lawyer Leo Spitz, who, before handing the money over, reached into the suitcase and pulled out $1,000 and stuffed it in his pocket "for carrying charges," he explained.

Like the small timers they were, after the payoff, Bioff and Brown went out on the town and gambled away thousands of dollars in a mob-run casino inside the Loop, a place called the Club 100, run by Nick Circella, a surly hood who worked directly for syndicate boss Frankie Rio, a former Capone bodyguard. Rio and Circella were in the club that night, both of them had known Bioff for twenty years. As they sipped their espressos from the owner's table, and watched Bioff lose another grand on the roulette wheel, Circella wondered aloud, "where two losers like Willie and Brown would get that kind of cash." Rio was thinking the same thing and ordered Circella to find out what the two had been up to. Two days later, Frankie Rio called Bioff and Brown, and told them they were going to see Frank Nitti's home.

Circella

After the federal government railroaded Al Capone off to prison and out of power forever, his place was taken by Frank "The Enforcer" Nitti, who got the position more out of attrition due to thinning mob ranks than anything else. Bioff and Brown, dressed in their best suits, waited in the drawing room of Nitti's twenty-room mansion, having arrived 15 minutes early. George Brown was terrified. He was certain the summons to Nitti's place was the kiss of death, although he didn't know what he done to deserve it. But Bioff, always the smarter of the two, saw the summons for what it was, the opportunity. Otherwise, he reasoned, if they had crossed Nitti in some way they didn't realize, they would have been dead already, left in a back alley in the loop someplace, not waiting in a living room on a Saturday morning.

After a half hour, a young, smartly dressed thug they didn't recognize came out and led them into a large, formal living room where Phil D'Andrea, former Capone bodyguard, Paul Ricca, Charles "Cherry Nose" Gioe, a top executive in the outfit and Louis "Little New York" Campagna were waiting. The boss himself, Frank Nitti, sat in his desk chair, glaring up at Brown and Bioff. "Where'd you get the money?" Nitti snapped. "And don't you fuck'n lie to me."

Campagna

George Brown was too terrified to speak, so Bioff did all the talking, explaining the entire shakedown in a matter of minutes, but blaming everything on his partner, George Brown. Nitti understood everything, even before Bioff had finished talking. He also saw the big picture at once. There were hundreds of movie theaters in pre-television Chicago, thousands in Illinois and tens of thousands across the United States.

The potential was endless. Nitti leaned back in his oversized leather chair and declared that he was cutting the outfit in on B&B's deal for 50%, although he would later increase that to 75% and then 90%. From that amount, 10% of the gross went into the mob's general treasury and the rest was divided up among those who had invested in the scheme. Furthermore, Nitti said, he was taking the stagehand's union from Bioff and Brown and reducing them to his bagmen within the union. They, Brown and Bioff, would handle the day-to-day problems in the local, but if they had any serious troubles, they were to report them to Nick Circella. When he was finished talking, Nitti leaned up towards his desk and said, "All right, now get out."

The Chicago outfit had always had its eye on Hollywood. It started with Capone. Just before he went to jail forever, Big Al had called a general meeting of the boys and told them he intended to extend his power westward to Los Angeles and ordered Nitti to draw up a plan to look into taking over Chicago's enormous entertainment industry. Then the Taxmen came around and slammed away Capone for good, but Nitti never forgot the plan to invade Hollywood. Now, in 1933, Nitti looked at Hollywood and its stars and producers with skeletons in their closets, and said, "The goose was in the oven waiting to be cooked."

He was right, too. Los Angeles was a wide-open city. Disputes were settled in gunshots, wildcat gangsters simply moved into town and bribed politicians, elections were rigged by competing gangs. The district attorney, Baron Fritts, was already on his way to becoming one of the country's most corrupt lawmen and the police chief, Jim Davis, was a loudmouth clown who carried two six-gun revolvers, and, was so corrupt that a detective's badge could be purchased for five dollars. The Mayor, Frank Shaw, admitted to newspapers that he rigged elections and placed his brother in charge of a spy squad within the police department that kept track of, and intimidated, his enemies. Compared to Los Angeles, Frank Nitti's Chicago was a bastion of order. But that was Los Angeles. Hollywood was a different place, hell it was a different planet.

An avid reader of the daily financials, Nitti learned that the movie business was ripe for extortion, for a wage increase shakedown, because the depression had hit the industry hard, and profits were off. The danger in low profits for the studios, was that the entire motion picture business was only 15 years old.

Other, older and more established businesses might be able to withstand a drain on its cash, but the Hollywood studios weren't ready for the same trial. Still, even with sagging profits and a shaky foundation, movie pictures were one of America's top ten grossing industries. Every day, tens of millions of dollars poured into its bank accounts, and Nitti and the syndicate wanted a piece of the cash. With control of the national union entertainment unions, they would get it, just the way Capone had planned it back in 1929. A few days after the meeting with Brown and Bioff, Frank Nitti met with his council at the Capri restaurant inside Chicago's loop so he could introduce his plan to take over the entire union on a national level.

Over lunch, Nitti pulled out the newspaper clipping he had on Balaban's nationwide operation and said he had spent the morning on the phone with Lucky Luciano in New York. He told the boys, Paul Ricca, Louis Campagna, Frankie Rio and Nick Circella, that he and Luciano had decided that their mobs, New York and Chicago, would work together to take over the movie business across America.

The entertainment business was too big, Nitti explained, and covered too many miles, for Chicago to try and take it alone. Besides, he added, Luciano and the other New York families already controlled the East Coast Stage Workers and projectionists' locals whose control was vital to a successful takeover. Nitti said that he and Lucky had decided that the first place to start was with Barney Balaban. They would send Bioff back into Balaban's office with a demand for a 20% increase for the projectionists. Nitti said that he expected Balaban to refuse to pay. When he did, the New York syndicate, working the Chicago syndicate, would arrange a general strike against all of Balaban's theaters on the East Coast and the Midwest.

Nitti said that the projectionists would be out of work for a few weeks and the theater chain would close down. Then, at the last minute, Nitti would send in George Brown to act as peacemaker and stabilizer who would end the strike through peaceful negotiations, while at the same time getting the projectionists a small raise. With that done, the mob would run him for the Stagehand Union presidency in the next election. That's what they did and it worked. The strike ended and George Brown was the hero of the working man and the studios alike.

In June of 1934, the union held its national election in Louisville, Kentucky. With the weight of the entire national syndicate behind him, George Brown was elected national President of the IATSE, the union that, effectively, controlled the entertainment business, and Willie Bioff was appointed Brown's "Special Representative", at a salary of $22,000. The Chicago mob's takeover of a giant American industry had begun. After the convention, Frank Nitti called Bioff and Brown into his office and told them that he had decided that it was best if they, Bioff and Brown, moved out to California where they would be closer to the studio's offices and production centers. The pair did as they were ordered, and while Brown spent most his time locked behind his office doors drinking beer, Willie Bioff made himself busy. In less than three months, he took $250,000 in cash from the movie moguls at Warner, 20th Century Fox, Paramount, everybody paid, all of it in cash, wrapped in brown paper bundles.

When the Chicago outfit moved in on Hollywood, the only person out west who was truly happy about the move was Johnny Roselli, because finally, after fifteen years of being exiled to the West coast, Roselli's star was starting to shine. Roselli was Chicago's sleeper agent out west, having been sent there in late 1924, to develop gambling, extortion and vice rackets for the outfit, and to help set up a national wire service, which was run by Moses Annenberg, whose family would later publish TV Guide.

The outfit's choice (actually it was Al Capone's decision) to send Johnny Roselli to Hollywood was a smart one, because Johnny was a real hustler, an "earner," with movie star good looks, an easy charm and a smooth but phony style that fit right into the Hollywood scene of the fifties and sixties. But despite his polished manner, expensive suits and practiced dialogue, Roselli was nothing more than a slicked-back hood, an antisocial punk with deep, psychological problems that put a permanent chip on his shoulders. Prison doctors labeled him an extreme paranoid.

Roselli

An illegal immigrant into the United States, Roselli always claimed he didn't know his birth date, instead celebrating his birthday on July 4, since it was "easy to remember and comes around at the same time every year." He said he thought he was born in 1905, but he couldn't remember where; it was all a lie of course, because when it came to his personal business, Johnny Roselli lied all the time. Roselli knew exactly when he was born, June 4, 1905, and where he was born, as Filippo Sacco in Esteria, Italy.

He came to Boston, illegally, when he was 6 years old. His first brush with the law came on September 14, 1922, when Roselli was trailed by federal narcotic agents as he delivered a quarter ounce bag of morphine to a drug addict named Fisher who was also a government informant. Roselli was arrested, but made bail.

The case was eventually dropped because the state's witness, Fisher, had disappeared and was believed to have been killed. He was also an arsonist. After his drug arrest, Roselli and his step father, hoping to finance a trip back to their native Italy tried to burn their house down to collect on the fire insurance but the

Fire Department reacted too quickly and put the fire out.

After that, Roselli went to New York and started running bootleg booze and acting as a guard, protecting beer wagons as they rolled through the streets of Manhattan. It was at that point, probably in or about the middle of 1923, that Roselli was recruited out to Chicago by the Capone organization which was in the middle of yet another territory war. Likable, smart and handsome, Roselli eventually managed to get close to Al Capone's inner circle, at one point he was even reported to be Capone's cousin, which is how other hoods explained the relationship, but the connection may have been Roselli's ability to provide Capone with a steady flow of cocaine out of New York.

While in Chicago, Roselli leafed through an encyclopedia and found the name Cosimo Roselli, a fifteenth-century painter who contributed frescoes of Moses on Mount Sinai and the Last Super on the walls of the Sistine Chapel. Impressed, and in need of a new name anyway, Roselli kept his first name, John, and took on the last name, Roselli. Eventually. Capone shared his lifelong dream with Roselli, to move west to Los Angeles, then still a mostly rural but growing community, and rebuild the mob out there. Roselli had always wanted to move to California, in fact when he was a boy he had dreams of settling their with his mother, so when Johnny Torrio, the leader of the Chicago outfit in 1925, and Al Capone, talked to Roselli about spearheading their move out west, Johnny was all for it.

Roselli's first two years out west were rough. He was sick and gaunt from tuberculosis, and penniless since all that the Chicago outfit had going out in California were high hopes and big plans, but no money producing operations. Then, in 1926, Roselli went to work for Anthony "The Hat" Cornero a colorful if slightly off-balance southern California bootlegger and gambler. Prohibition had made Cornero rich and Roselli profited as a result.

For the first time in his life, Roselli had enough money to rent a house outside of the Italian ghettos he had known since moving to America. He bought a car, started to dress better, and, as the bootlegger and bookmaker to a growing number of movie stars, he started to move in higher circles.

Zwillman

It was Cornero who recommended Roselli to Longy Zwillman, the New Jersey labor rackets boss who had expanded his criminal empire into the most successful rum-running enterprise on the East coast. Zwillman was a Hollywood regular and met with Roselli often, grew to like him and came to rely on him as his primary West coast contact and even assigned Roselli to watch over the various starlets that Zwillman dated. In turn, Zwillman put other big name East coast hoods in touch with Roselli as the man to see when they went west, and when Capone traveled to Los Angeles in 1927, Roselli showed him around the city and introduced him to movie stars, which impressed the movie stars and Capone, and gave Roselli a lot of prestige around town. Roselli also remembered Capone's visit and talked about it often over the years. He said that even for California's laid-back lifestyle of the twenties, Capone's banana yellow suits and shocking pink silk shoes, "pimp gear" he called it, were outrageous. He remembered that the press, crowds and the police hounded them everywhere and Capone seemed to love all the attention. Roselli would remember it for the rest of his life and the smart crook that he was, he learned from it.

Capone

He shunned Capone's type of flamboyance. He learned to fit in with the

Hollywood crowd, but to keep a low profile, and aside from an arrest in Los Angeles in 1925 for carrying a concealed weapon, Roselli was virtually unknown to law enforcement.

After Capone went to jail, Roselli was still out in Los Angeles, exiled as he saw it, and considering a career in films. Then Frank Nitti called and told Johnny that his moment had come, the outfit was moving in on Hollywood and Roselli would lead the attack on the West Coast, the so-called Bioff scandal, that extorted millions out of the Hollywood studios in the mid-1930s. Convicted in scam, Roselli did a few years hard time and strutted out of jail on August 13, 1947.

The slick little hood leaped right back into the rackets and the center of Hollywood. Even while he was in prison, Roselli kept in touch with the Hollywood community by way of his friend, talent agent Danny Winkler, who wrote to him with the latest gossip, and from the 250 letters he received from a bit-part actress named Beatrice Ann Frank, who, in 1947, became Roselli's fiancée, but nothing ever came of it.

Eventually, Johnny did marry a promising young actress named June Lang, born June Valasek, who was 12 years younger than Roselli, was madly in love with him and had no idea that he was a gangster, because Roselli had told her he was an aspiring movie producer.

June Lang

But, with time, the truth came out, and Johnny promised her he would leave the rackets. But what he said, and what he did were two different things and soon, Lang came to see that Roselli would never change and divorced him. After that, Johnny dated actors Betty Hutton, Lana Turner and Donna Reed, among many others, and still managed to find time to have an affair with Bugsy Siegel's girlfriend, Virginia Hill, but that may have been ordered by Paul Ricca back in Chicago, so that Hill and Roselli would spy on each other.

Lang and Roselli

Amazingly, producer Joe Schenck, just out of prison himself as a result of the Bioff mess, sponsored Roselli for a job at Eagle Lion Studios, a small, British owned production company, where the hood worked with Brian Foy, Vice President in charge of production. Eagle-Lion churned out a dozen true life, fast paced, low budget crime related semi-documentary films, which Foy clipped out of the tabloid papers.

Bryan Foy

The Docudramas were popular with critics and fans alike, and lead the way for television police dramas like Dragnet. Roselli would work at Eagle Lion, on the records anyway, as a purchasing agent for $50 a week and would be "promoted," by Foy of course, through the ranks, to associate producer. It was the only legitimate job Roselli ever had and apparently he had a knack for the business, and produced several hit films for Eagle-Lion, including the dark gangster dramas, which now have a cult status, "He Walked By Night," "T-Men," and "Canon City."

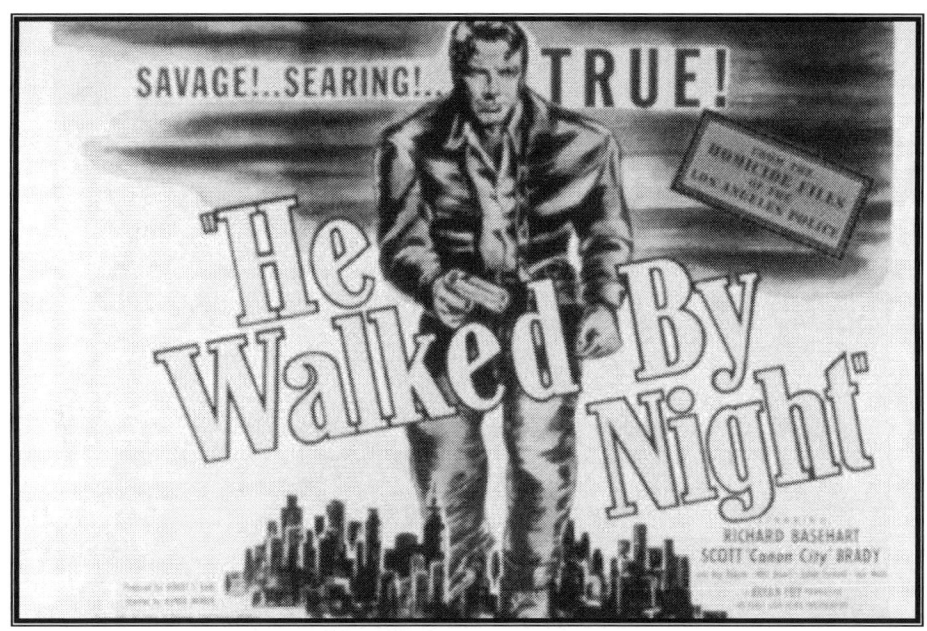

Roselli's other official source of income, outside of the Studios, was as an agent for Nationwide, the only wire service into California and wholly owned and operated by the mob, although he was supplementing his income by replacing Willie Bioff as the DuPont Film Corporation's representative to Hollywood. Actually, Roselli probably knew nothing at all about film stock, but the outfit still controlled large parts of the studios and if DuPont wanted to remain a dominant force in Hollywood, it had to cooperate and leave Roselli on the payroll. DuPont never complained since Roselli had so much influence with the studio bosses and the company wanted to take the Hollywood film market from Eastman-Kodak, who had a virtual lock on the market.

Roselli was also the Chicago outfit's West Coast executioner of choice, and since territory battles for control of Los Angeles continued on into the early 1970s, Roselli did, as Jimmy "The Weasel" Fratianno, an LA mob boss turned informant said, "a lot of work when he was a kid. He did a lot of fuck'n work, don't worry." Otherwise, Roselli kept his standard low profile and shunned publicity. But, flush with cash, Roselli allowed himself one little bit of color, he moved into Hollywood's famous Garden of Allah, then a swinging bungalow complex that was home to dozens of stars, from Humprey Bogart to Edward G. Robinson. But Roselli's move into the heart of stardom was no mistake either.

Jimmy "The Weasel" Fratianno at work

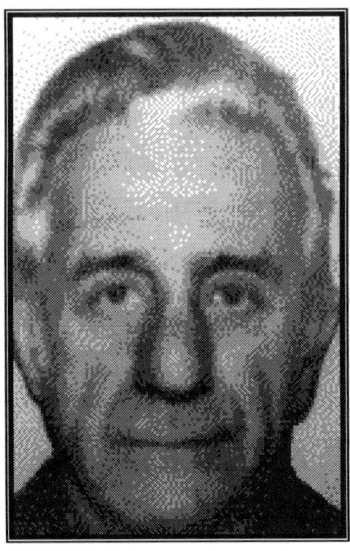

The Two Tonys—Brancato and Trombino, were a cowboy-mobsters from Kansas City. In May 1951 they robbed the cash room at the mob owned and operated Flamingo Hotel in Las Vegas. The two Tony's and three others robbed the placed dressed alike and wearing large fedora hats. However in mid-robbery, Tony Brancato dropped his hat and was caught on camera. The casino Mobsters recognized him and sent out a hit team to kill and Trombino. At the same time, the FBI placed Brancato on the Ten Most Wanted List. The FBI eventually arrested them in connection to a robbery in Beverly Hills, but released them on bail after which the Two Tony's split for Los Angeles and started to shake down mob connected bookie. LA Jack Dragna decided to end it all for them. He ordered Aladena Fratianno, aka Jimmy the Weasel, to take of the situation. Fratianno reached out to the two hoods and told them he wanted their help in robbing a high stakes poker game. They took the Weasel up on his offer and agreed to wait for him on Hollywood Boulevard. When they arrived, on August 6, 1951, Fratianno and two of his men gunned them down.

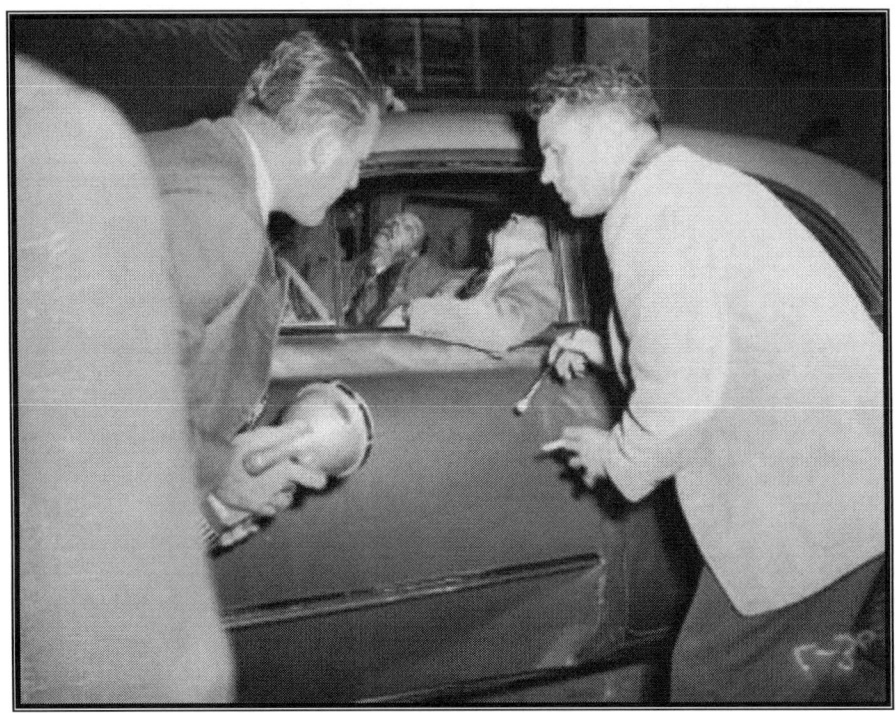

Johnny was also one of Hollywood's leading loan sharks, was ordered by Chicago to spread out as much mob influence among the stars and the people who ran the studios as he could, either with money or drugs, and since most of the big stars were constantly overspending themselves, his loan sharking business grew at phenomenal rates.

Over three decades, Roselli estimated that he had loaned out at least five million dollars in cash to some of Hollywood's leading stars and producers, from Ronald Reagan to Ed Sullivan and dozens of others. Roselli was also the Chicago outfit's talent scout, finding promising actresses or actors, and then sponsoring their careers in Tinseltowns. According to Johnny, it was the Chicago outfit that sponsored the Marx Brothers, George Raft, Jimmy Durante, Marie McDonald, Clark Gable, Gary Cooper, Jean Harlow, Gary Grant and Wendy Barrie and as a result were awarded extravagant contracts by the studios. The next logical step was to control the talent outlets, so in the late 1940s, when the mob's Vegas casinos discovered that live entertainment brought in the crowds, Roselli and the mob opened a talent booking agency called Monte Prosser Productions, which was the only agency used by all Vegas casinos. Roselli ran the company of his apartment at the Desert Inn, and had such a firm grip on Vegas' entertainment, that he even had the contract to represent the company that put the ice machine in all the hotels.

Roselli and Foy, despite Foy's financial success at Eagle-Lion studios, were both let go because of Foy's brash, confrontational style that annoyed the studio brass, and when his three-year contract expired in 1950 he was released and Roselli was booted out with him. Foy bounced over to Warner Brothers studios but couldn't take Roselli with him since the studio had, officially anyway, barred Johnny from the lot. But Foy remained close with Roselli: "They were like the Rover boys," Foy's niece said, "they went everywhere together."

The pair spent most of their weekends at Foy's house, where there was also a party. At one of those weekend parties, Foy introduced Roselli to one of his favorite contract players at Warner, Bill Campbell, who lived in the same apartment complex as Roselli.

Bill Campbell

Campbell was married to a stunning young actress named Judy Campbell, who was born Judith Eileen Katherine Immoor in Pacific Palisades in 1934.

Judy Campbell

She had met Campbell when she was 16, and married him two years later in 1952. Bill Campbell became fast friends and Campbell introduced Roselli to his wife. Like most men who met her, Roselli was awestruck at Campbell's beauty and taken with her quick wit and disarming charm.

Sinatra and Jackie Kennedy

After Judy divorced Campbell in 1954, Roselli introduced Judy to Frank Sinatra in late 1959 and a year later, Sinatra introduced Campbell to both John Kennedy and Mob Boss Sam Giancana.

It was about this same time, in 1960-61, that Roselli became embroiled in the Mafia-CIA-White House plots to kill Cuba's Castro. It was interesting that one day in early 1975, film producer Bernie Foy called Johnny Roselli with the idea of doing a remake of the movie "The Exorcist."

In the new version, a nun would be possessed by the devil who would then drive her to acts of sexual depravity. Roselli read the script, but rejected it as sacrilegious. However, Roselli then pitched his own idea for a film. The story concerned a patriotic mobster who becomes entangled in a White House-CIA plot to assassinate Fidel Castro. However, the scheme backfired when Castro hires his own mobsters to kill the American President. Foy and his financial backers heard out the Roselli pitch and then rejected it as too implausible.

Sinatra, Kennedy Brother-in-Law Peter Lawford and RFK

In 1966, Johnny Roselli arranged for St. Louis Mafia Don Anthony Giordano and the caporegime in Detroit, Anthony Zerilli, to buy hidden assets in the Frontier Hotel.

Anthony Zerilli

It was an otherwise uneventful, commonplace underworld deal. Johnny collected his $100,000 finder fee and that was the end of it. Then a Federal grand jury called Roselli in for questioning about his years in Las Vegas. Roselli refused to testify on the grounds that he could incriminate himself, so the grand jury gave him immunity, and Roselli talked, although in the end, he really didn't give the jury anything against anybody.

Anthony Giordano

Unfortunately for Roselli, his testimony was stamped secret, so when Giordano and Zerilli were convicted of hiding their assets in the Frontier Hotel, the sale that Roselli had arranged, it looked like Johnny had talked. After that, he was a dead man. But before anything could be done, Roselli and four others were indicted for running a card cheating hustle at the Friars Club in Beverly Hills, where Roselli was a member, having been sponsored by the club's founder, Georgie Jessel, Dean Martin, and, of course, Frank Sinatra. Roselli thanked them by setting up a high stakes gin rummy game that included Phil Silvers, Zeppo Marx, and Tony Martin, the millionaire husband to Debbi Reynolds. Unknown to them Roselli had a "peeper" hidden behind a wall at the tables who transmitted the players' hands electronically to Roselli. When the scam was exposed, one of Roselli's spotters in the game, George Sears, turned informant.

5 Found Guilty in Friars Club Card-Cheating Conspiracy Trial

BY GENE BLAKE
Times Staff Writer

All five defendants in the Friars Club card-cheating conspiracy case were found guilty Monday on all 49 felony counts after a federal court trial of nearly six months.

A jury of 10 women and two men returned the verdicts before U.S. Dist. Judge William P. Gray, cul-

Alleged bribery investigated in Friars case. See Page 3, Part 1.

minating about 22 hours of deliberations spread over four days.

Judge Gray set Jan. 20 for sentencing and hearing arguments on motions for acquittal, new trials

130 years for another, Maurice H. Friedman. Fines of $5,000 on some counts and $10,000 on others also could be imposed.

Benjamin J. Teitelbaum could receive up to 83 years, John Rosselli 43 years and Manuel (Ricky) Jacobs 38 years, along with fines.

A sixth defendant, Dr. Victor G. Lands, pleaded guilty to one count of falsifying an income tax return and did not stand trial. He also will be sentenced Jan. 20.

All five who went to trial were convicted of engaging in a five-year conspiracy to violate federal laws by cheating wealthy members of the exclusive Friars Club in Beverly Hills at gin rummy.

Roselli was arrested, found guilty and sentenced to five years at McNeil Island. In the meantime, the Organized Crime Unit within the Justice Department was planning to have him deported if he didn't start talking about his life in the outfit. This time Roselli talked.

He was released from prison, but he was broke and borrowing money to get by and in the last half of 1974, he was forced to move into his sister's house in Florida and that's where they caught up with him.

Johnny Roselli was last seen in the company of the two men getting aboard a private yacht for a cruise. As he sat on the deck sipping a drink, one of the men slipped behind him and choked him to death with a white nylon rope. Then they taped a washcloth over his mouth, sawed off his legs at the thigh with a hand saw, stuffed him into a 55 gallon drum that was weighed down with chains. The coroner figured that the killer also shot him and then decided to dig the bullet out of his body before they dumped him in the barrel and then dumped it into the bay. Body gases pushed the body onto the surface ten days later.

Auippa

Several weeks later, during a meeting with the boys, Chicago's acting boss, Joey Auippa summed up the measure of Roselli's life with the outfit: "You remember that guy from the old days, that guy ... what the fuck was his name ... that guy they found in the barrel down there inside of Florida? What do you think of that?" There was a moment's silence until somebody across the room cracked, "Johnny in a drum."

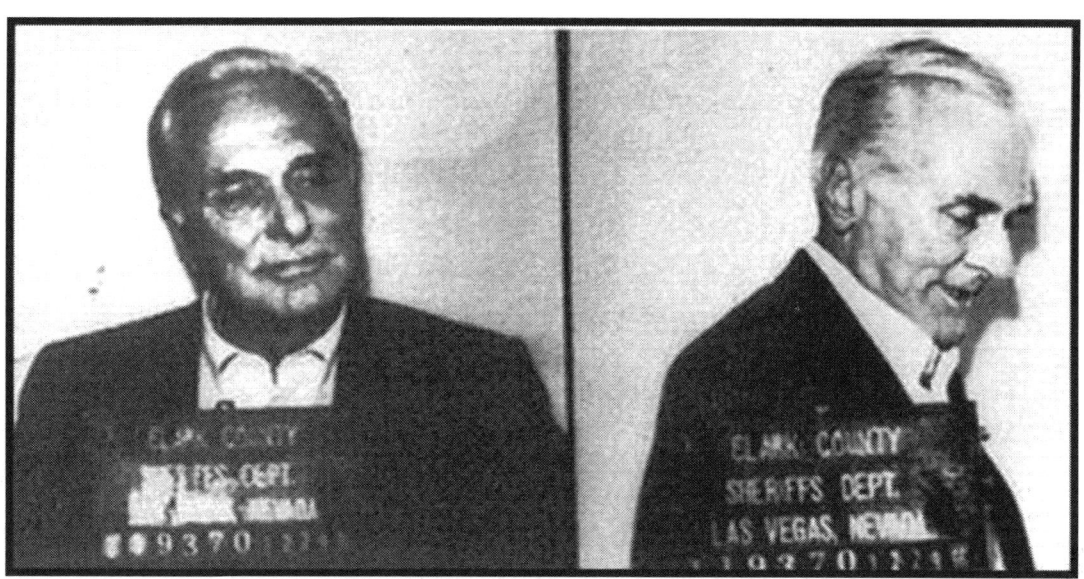

Roselli

When Willie Bioff arrived in Hollywood, Roselli met him at the train station and gave the little pimp an orientation tour of the city and the industry he was about to bring to its knees. As they drove through Beverly Hills, Roselli stopped in front of Joan Crawford's mansion and told Bioff an interesting story. Roselli said that right after he had landed a job for himself as a staff investigator for the Hay's office, he was given a case to look into by MGM Studios. It seemed that when one of their rising stars, a real beauty named Joan Crawford, was a starving 19-year-old actress, she had appeared in several pornographic films. Now in 1935, some freelance extortionists said that they had a print of the film and were shaking down MGM for $100,000 to hand over the film negative.

Willie Bioff

The bosses over at MGM considered the investment they already had in Crawford, added that with her box office appeal and potential, and decided that it would be less expensive to pay the extortionists off, but not for $100,000. The bosses handed the case over to Roselli and told him to contact the hoods and offer them $25,000 in cash to back off. The studio would write the money off of their taxes as a business expense.

Roselli contacted the hoods, a group of small timers, and explained that he represented not only MGM Studios but the Mafia as well. He told them that if they ever contacted the studios or Crawford again, he'd kill them. Case solved. Roselli pocketed the studio's $25,000, produced the film negative and the threats stopped.

A few years later, Roselli and Bioff met again. After a complicated series of federal wage laws and disputes with the movie studios over a 20% increase in salaries, the independent entertainment unions decided to strike on April 30, 1937. A strike by these unions could close down film production across California. If that happened, the syndicate would never collect on their control over the unions. The studios wanted the strike broken and they wanted the syndicate to break it. Frank Nitti argued against any involvement, but this time things were reversed, the studios pressured the outfit, and took their case to Lucky Luciano and Longy Zwillman in New York. Luciano and Zwillman talked to Nitti and, reluctantly, Nitti agreed to break the strike.

Zwillman

Nitti handed the job to Johnny Roselli who hired a squad of twenty leg-breakers from Chicago and San Francisco and marched them to the Hollywood police station where they were given gun permits and then brought them to the studio gates where the striking union membership was gathered. Armed with baseball bats and steel chains, Roselli's goons threw themselves at the striking union members who took a severe beating that first day but were back on the strike line the next morning.

The outfit goons continued to dole out beatings for several more weeks before the union brass imported its own sluggers, some hired from local gyms, others brought in from the Long Shoreman's union in New York. Herb Sorrell, a labor organizer for the union recalled that "there were numerous fights, and it was a rough strike. In the six weeks that it lasted, there were several killed and I didn't know how many injured.

In fact it was the roughest strike I ever participated in." Realizing that brute force wouldn't win the strike, Roselli told George Brown and Willie Bioff to call a press conference with the studio bosses and declare the striking union's leadership as "communist infiltrated." Then all-powerful Screen Actors Guild voted to ignore the union's picket lines and eventually the smaller unions either disbanded or became a part of the larger organizations.

Bioff

The Federation of Motion Picture Crafts was destroyed, the outfit's union reigned supreme. Nitti, who always expected the worst in everything, was amazed to find out that he didn't need a ramrod to knock down Hollywood's golden gates. He just knocked gently and they sprung open for him. The reason for that was that Hollywood, as Nitti would quickly learn, was, like him, all about money.

Although it later became known as the Bioff and Brown extortion scandal, it wasn't really extortion, at least not in the classic sense, because the studio heads, by paying off Bioff and Nitti's not to raise prices, were actually saving money, perhaps millions of dollars over what they would have to have paid a legitimate union in wage increases. Furthermore, the scandal benefited the studios in other ways because the mob, for everything that was evil about it, usually kept its word once it was paid, and the mob had agreed not to raise labor prices.

Bioff

That promise assured the studios that productions would finish without stoppage or a problem from IATSE's 12,000 members, and as result of a toothless union, the studios fired workers at will and pushed others to work over time without compensation; as a result, films were made for less money because not as many people were needed. In fact, the payoffs to the mob, saved the studios about $15,000,000.00 in what they would have paid out in wage increases.

With the mob behind them as a working partner, the studios no longer had to deal with Communists who had infiltrated the locals and stirred up trouble, or the small time thugs who kept coming back for more nickels and dimes or the weak labor leaders who couldn't keep their promises because they had no real control over their membership. Producers knew that with the mob in charge, they could get a picture wrapped up on schedule because there would be no strikes and as an added bonus the mob ordered Bioff & Brown to raise prices for live theater, opera, plays and concerts, which were competing with the movie business. Everybody, except the membership, was happy.

Joe Schenck

Joe Schenck was one of the founding Fathers of Hollywood. Joe Schenck got involved with, in fact he almost helped to design, the mob's shakedown of the Hollywood studios in April of 1936. Unlike the gangsters who lived from day to day on their incomes, the studio heads relied on budgets. Bioff's surprise visits were starting to tax the bottom line. The studio heads gathered together and decided to let Nick Schenck come up with a plan that would satisfy the outfit and the studios.

Schenck was about to pay Bioff anywhere near a million dollars, however, he did a quick take on Bioff and decided that he could be bribed. Schenck told Bioff that the DuPont representative in California wanted to increase his raw film business with MGM and the other studios. He said that DuPont was willing to pay Bioff a 7% commission to act as the designated "agent" between DuPont Chemical and the Hollywood studios; better yet, all of the actual footwork would be done by a "sub agent" assigned by DuPont, all Bioff had to do was cash the checks.

Bioff agreed to the deal under the conditions that his income never fell under $50,000 a year and that Schenck was not to mention the commission deal to anyone else, meaning Frank Nitti, or his west coast boy, Johnny Roselli. Schenck called the other studio heads, explained the situation and all of them agreed, reluctantly, to switch their business from Eastman Kodak raw film to DuPont. In the last part of 1937, the raw film commission deal that Schenck had put together gave Bioff $159,025 in commissions, an enormous amount of money for that time.

Flush with more cash than he ever dreamed possible, Willie Bioff "went Hollywood." He started to wear expensive clothes and carried three diamond-studded, solid gold, union business cards in his wallet. Using mostly union funds, and by applying yet another special collection on the studios, Bioff was able to raise enough funds to buy a massive ranch. Here, he grew alfalfa and flowers and relaxed in his mahogany-paneled mansion where, although he could barely read, Bioff had a pine-knot library filled with the world's greatest books and rare and expensive volumes.

He bought a Louis XV bedroom and rare Chinese vases and fancied himself a connoisseur of rare vases and had a kidney shaped swimming pool built in the back yard for his seven children. Willie Bioff's new ranch and the unusual methods he used to finance it weren't missed by Montgomery Clift, the Screen

Actors Guild President, who had his own informants within the studios. Clift figured, correctly, that the ranch was a payoff from Schenck to ensure Bioff's secrecy. Then, one of Clift's informants provided him with a copy of the check that Schenck had made out to Willie Bioff for $100,000. Clift reported the deal to the IRS and eventually Schenck was secretly indicted for tax evasion. When questioned about the check he had written to Bioff, Schenck said it was a loan. Later on, he made the mistake of testifying to that under oath. When the government was able to prove that Schenck paid Bioff the money as a means to avoid taxes, he was indicted on several counts of tax evasion. Schenck, always the businessman, decided to cooperate with the government in exchange for his a light sentence.

The government agreed and Joe Schenck sat before the grand jury and outlined the entire scam. The grand jury eventually found Schenck guilty of tax evasion and he was sentenced to five years at a federal prison, but Joe Schenck wasn't just anybody. He wasn't going to serve out his term in jail and the whole world knew it.

He served just under a year, was granted a Presidential by Harry S. Truman and then went to running his studios as though nothing had happened. Based on Schenck's testimony, the federal grand jury issued subpoenas for all the major studio heads, but still, up until almost the very end, the government had no real clear understanding of the extent of Bioff's extortion scam or the fact that the mob, New York and Chicago, were involved. Then Harry Warner stood before the grand jury and filled in the gaps. Warner's evidence was enough to put everybody involved behind bars.

Left to right: Cherry Nose Gioe, Phil D'Andrea, and Campagna. Paul Ricca is the second man from the right

On May 23, 1941, Brown, Bioff, Paul Ricca, Frank Nitti, Nick Circella, Charlie Gioe, and Phil D'Andrea were indicted for extortion and tax evasion. Willie Bioff had no intention of doing any jail time. He called US Attorney Boris Kostelanetz from a jailhouse visitor's phone and opened the conversation by saying, "This is Bioff . . . Okay, Boris, what do you want to know?" Bioff laid out the entire scheme for Kostelanetz, times, dates, places, names and amounts; of course he worked a good deal for himself first. In exchange for his testimony, the government agreed to let Bioff keep the money he had stolen over the past decade, furthermore, he would walk away from any charges against him.

After three weeks, Bioff finished giving his testimony to the grand jury, and when he was finished talking, indictments were handed down for Johnny Roselli, Frank Nitti, Paul Ricca, Louis Campagna, Charlie Gioe, Phil D'Andrea, Ralph Pierce and Frankie Diamond. There was a trial, but none of the outfit members took the stand in their own defense, the case against them was that overwhelming. On December 30, 1943, the verdict against them was returned. They were each found guilty and sentenced an average of ten years in federal prison plus $10,000 fine and were liable for the back taxes owed. It was, as the Chicago Herald American wrote, "The total demolition of the Chicago syndicate."

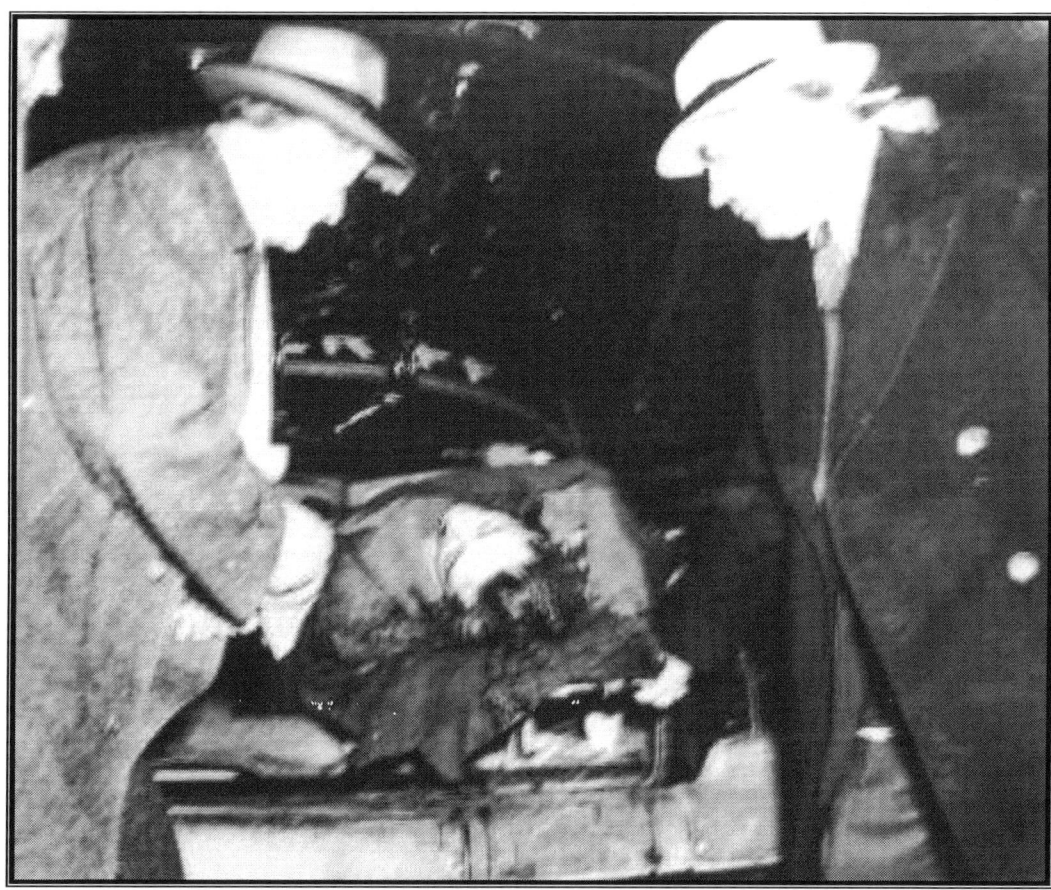

Frank Nitti, Dead

Frank Nitti never went to trial on the Bioff charges, because a day before he was indicted, he took a .45 and blew his brains out, just as he had always promised he would if he ever faced another long prison sentence. Paul Ricca decided he wasn't going to do any jail time either. Working through Campagna's wife they were put in touch with a Missouri legislator named Edward "Putty Nose" Brady who in turn placed them in contact with a St. Louis lawyer named Paul Dillon who wasn't new to the mob.

He knew Murray Humphreys, the Chicago outfit's collector, very well and had defended two IATSE union officers at Humphreys' request, after they were caught beating up a movie theater owner in St. Louis in 1939. Dillon, then 68, also had strong political connections to the Missouri underworld including Johnny Lazia, the Kansas City gambling king who was killed in 1934 and Tom Pendergast, the boss of Kansas City. But, what Ricca needed Dillon for was his close, personnel relationship with President Harry Truman.

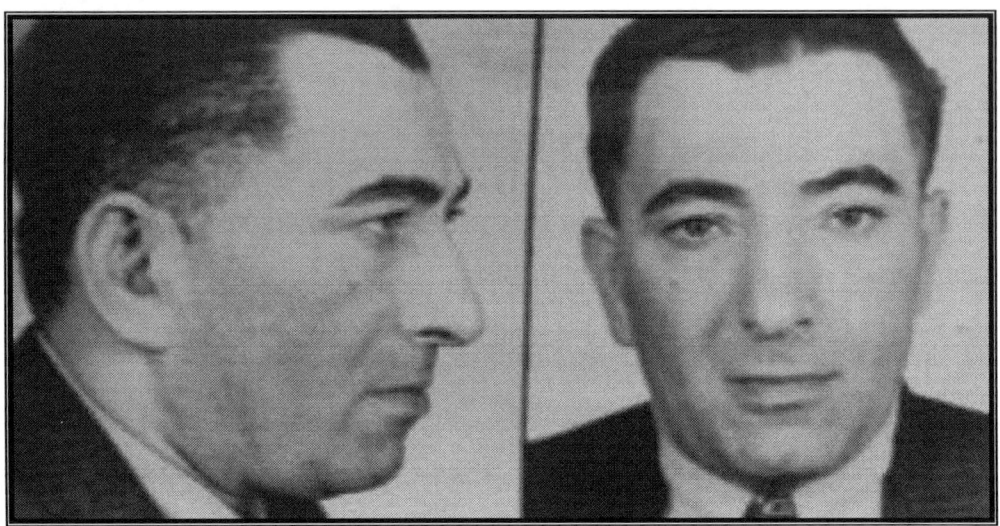

John Lanza

In 1934, at the personnel request of Missouri crime king, Boss Pendergast, Dillon had acted as Harry Truman campaign manager in his race for the senate. Dillon had also worked as a lawyer for Boss Pendergast, and represented Pendergasts's chief lieutenant, "Smiling Johnny" Lazia, on an income tax fraud charge. Dillon loved the power, the money and the clout working with these clients gave him. He bragged, often and loudly, that he could visit Truman at the White House whenever he wanted to.

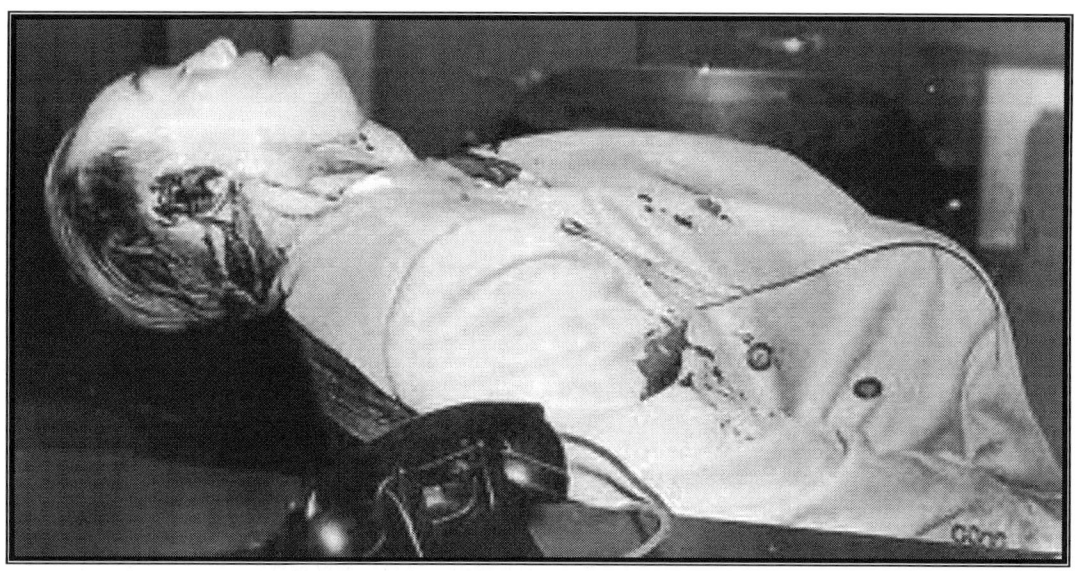

"Brother Johnny" Lanza dead, killed by the Mob in 1934

In October of 1945, Dillon met "Putty Nose" Brady, who had ties to the Chicago outfit that went back to the Capone organization. With Brady at the meeting was an ex-prizefighter, and occasional Brady business partner, James Testa. Dillon, according to Testa, provided them with a price list with a set amount of money he would need to have each of the Chicago hoods released by using his influence in Washington with the Truman White House. While Dillon was collecting his bribe money from Testa and Brady, another lawyer named Maury Hughes of Dallas, traveled to Washington and met with Attorney General Clark. The two men had grown up together. Shortly after the meeting, the Attorney General requested the gangsters transfer to Leavenworth.

Tom Clark

For decades no one in law enforcement was clear on what hand Clark had played in the transfer or where Hughes fit in until Murray Humphreys summed it all up when he, knowingly or unknowingly, told an FBI microphone on October 16, 1964. "Attorney General Tom Clarke was, he always was, 100% for doing favors . . . the guy Maury Hughes who went to Clarke was an ex law partner (from Dallas) and then the scandal broke." Humphreys also said that another lawyer they hired, Bradley Eben, was paid the astounding fee of $15,000, an enormous amount of money in 1945, to "consult" on the case. Eben's mother was a Truman White House employee who worked as a liaison between Attorney General Clarke and the President.

Murray Humphreys

On August 6, 1947, Dillon, made an application for parole for Ricca, Gioe, Campagna and D'Andrea. The application was strongly opposed by Boris Kostelanetz, the special assistant attorney general, even the federal judge who passed sentence wrote to the attorney general Clark objecting to the application for parole. But, on August 13, 1947, exactly one week after the application for parole had been placed, Ricca, Campagna, Gioe and D'Andrea were released on parole. A three man, federal parole team voted unanimously to release the hoods and acted so quickly and quietly on their decision, that the parole office in Chicago didn't have time to submit its standard analysis of the case, which meant that the parole team reached its decision having seen only a fraction of the inmates' records.

The public, especially in Hollywood and Chicago, were outraged over the hoods' release, and Representative Fred E. Busbey confronted the Parole Board members and asked them, directly and without mincing words, if it was true that they had accepted a $500,000 bribe to grant paroles to the hoods. Remarkably, not one of the parole board members denied accepting the money, nor would they admit to it.

Fred E. Busbey

The House Expenditures Committee recommended that the four hoods be sent back to prison and that their paroles be revoked. The carefully worded report held that the paroles had been given under highly questionable circumstances, and identified Dillon and Hughes as being personal friends of President Truman and Attorney General Clark. It concluded, however, that it could find no grounds to indict the President, Clarke or Hughes and could find no evidence that anyone had been bribed but concluded that "A good Samaritan" had spent big money to get the hoods released.

That "good Samaritan" turned out to be Tony Accardo, who ordered each of his capos to visit the attorney's office and drop a specific amount on the desk to free Ricca and the others. They were to say nothing except, "This is for Paul Ricca," drop the money on the desk, and leave. By the end of the day, Ricca's lawyers had the $200,000 needed to pay off his tax lien. Now the hoods' Attorney could truly say that "a bunch of strangers and good and concerned citizens donated the money." When Louis Campagna was called before committee he said he didn't know who any of the estimated forty-two men were who dropped the money on the lawyer's desk or what their motivation was.

Campagna (right) with Paul Ricca

"Do you believe in Santa Claus?" Representative Hoffman asked Campagna.

"Yes, Yes. After all this," Campagna said "I suppose I do . . . I mean if you were me, wouldn't you?"

In its final report, the Congressional Committee charged to look into the entire mess wrote: "The syndicate has given the most striking demonstration of political clout in the history of the republic."

Willie Bioff moved to Arizona, where he lived under the name Willie Nelson, Nelson being his wife's maiden name. Contrary to what's usually written, Willie Bioff wasn't hiding out in Arizona. In fact, he worked at the Riviera Casino in Vegas as the entertainment director for Gus Greenbaum, Chicago's man in Nevada.

Outgoing, likable and very rich, Willie was a natural for politics, and was soon popular within the golden elite of Phoenix society, which is how he met Barry Goldwater, in November of 1952. The two men became fast friends. Goldwater, a brigadier general in the Air Force Reserve, flew Bioff and his wife all over the state to attend various parties, and Willie landed a steady flow of cash into Goldwater's political campaign chest. Bioff even loaned Bobby Goldwater $10,000 for a farming investment in Southern California.

A month before the Mafia killed him, Willie Bioff and his wife, Barry Goldwater and his family, vacationed together in Las Vegas. In 1955, Peter Licavoli and Paul Ricca, boss of the Chicago mob, started to shake Bioff down for cash. Willie paid off for a while, but then remarked that he might go to the federal government for help. The next morning, Bioff stepped into his Ford pickup, stepped on the gas and was killed instantly by a bomb planted under the hood of the truck. Both of his legs and his right arm was blown off.

Rand, Tamara. In November of 1975 Frank Bompensiro helped Anthony Spilotro locate millionaires San Diego real estate broker and investor Tamara Rand (Born 1921) a gynecologist.

Allen Glick

Allen Glick, the Outfits front man in Vegas, was being pressured by Tamara Rand to make good on what she said was a promise he made to her, following a $2 million loan. Essentially, Rand was shaking Glick down. Glick had struck in rich in Vegas and Rand felt she was entitled to a part of his money and threatened legal action if she didn't get it. Tony Spilotro found Rand in her Mission Hills California home shooting her once in the temple, once in the back and three times under the chin with a .22, Spilotro's weapon of choice. She was sipping tea when he killed her.

Rocco Alex (born Alexander Federico Petricone, Jr. on February 29, 1936) A well-known actor, (Rocco played the part of Moe Greene, a Las Vegas casino owner, in the film The Godfather.) Rocco was born in Somerville, Massachusetts where he was known to friends as Bobo. Rocco was vaguely connected through friends to the mostly Irish-American Winter Hill Gang in Boston.

Alex Rocco

On Labor Day weekend 1961, Rocco (Who then went by his given name Petricone) was at a "Time" a street party with his girlfriend when George McLaughlin of the rival the Charlestown Mob, tried to pick up Rocco's girlfriend. A fist fight erupted and the Winter Hill gang sent McLaughlin to the hospital and so began Boston's so-called Irish Wars that lasted through most of the 1960s.

The war ended with what was, essentially, the eradication of the Charlestown Mob. Rocco was suspected fled to California but was suspected of playing a role in the murder of Bernie McLaughlin.

San Francisco Mob: Francesco Lanza was the first Mafia boss in San Francisco, coming to power there during the prohibition. Police suspect that between April 28, 1928 and May 18, 1932, Lanza either murdered or ordered the murders of at least seven independent bootleggers. Prohibition and a lack of competition made Lanza rich. He operated the Fisherman's Warf and held interests in other legitimate firms as well. Lanza died on July 14, 1937 and his operations were taken over by Tony Lima. It was Lima who probably ordered his underboss Michael Abati to murder Chicago gangster Nick DeJohn.

In 1947, Jack Ruby, the man who murdered Lee Harvey Oswald, was reportedly involved with de John and Chicago hoods Paul Labriola, Marcus Lipsky and Paul Jones in an effort to take over gambling in the Texas area. Dejohn and two others cheated Chicago out of a sizable percentage of their gambling proceeds from the

Outfits operations in Texas, where DeJohn was located. DeJohn fled to Santa Rosa, California where he lived quietly away from the rackets. In the meantime, his two partners in the cheating scam were murdered. One was tossed down a storm drain, the other was found, frozen and shot dead, in the trunk of his own car.

One night in May of 1947, DeJohn stupidly left the safety of his home to dine at La Rocca's restaurant at the corner of Columbus and Taylor in San Francisco. His corpse was found the next morning in the trunk of his black Chrysler Town and Country at the Laguna and Greenwich. He'd been strangled with heavy braided fishing line. Both Tony Lima and Michael Abati were arrested but eventually the charges were dismissed. Police also locked up a local hood named Leonard Calamia, a known drug trafficker, but nothing came out of that arrest either. On April 27, 1953 Lima was sentenced to the California State Prison for grand theft. He never returned to power.

Michael Abati took over as boss in 1953 and remained boss until 1963. He attended the mob summit at Apalachin in November 1957 along with his underboss Joseph Lanza. Held by police during the raid, he was eventually deported back to Italy on July 8, 1961. He died there, of natural causes, on September 5, 1962.

Following Abati was Joseph Lanza AKA "Jimmy" who ran the family from 1961 through 1989. Lanza expanded the gang's power and influence into Vegas where it was represented by William "Bones' Remmer.

Lanza was also connected his family to Joe Cerrito of San Jose and Joseph Civello of Dallas and his underboss, Gaspare "Bill" Sciortino, was the first cousin to the underboss of the Los Angeles Samuel Sciortino. Police believe that it was Lanza who ordered the hit on New England family associate and government witness. Joseph "The Animal" Barboza. Lanza died in 1989. The gang managed to limp into the 21st century and is reported to be barely holding on.

San Jose/ San Diego Mob: In 1942, a hood named Onofrio Sciortino, a member of the Mafia, controlled loan sharking, gambling and prostitution in southern California. When Sciortino died on September 10, 1959, his underboss, Joey Cerrito, an Italian immigrant who arrived in California in the 1940s, took over.

Although not an influential power, Cerrito was one of the Mafia bosses caught in the November 1957 Apalachin Summit raid. In October of 1964, the US State Department identified Cerrito in Sicily meeting with Bonanno Consiglieri Frank Garofalo at a hotel in Palermo. The government speculated that the Bonanno was probably the cause of the meeting. When Cerrito died on September 8, 1978, his underlying Angelo Marino took over the gang. Marino kept close ties with the San Francisco and LA mobs. In 1977, Marino and his son were indicted for the murder of father and son, Orlando and Peter Catelli.

From what police have been able to piece together Catelli demanded a job in Marino California Cheese Company, which controlled 85% of the cheese distribution in California and 50% west of the Mississippi River. Marino refused and Catelli attempted to extort $100,000 from hm. In retaliation, Marino, ordered Catelli's father to kill him. The father refused so Marino had them both shot but the father survived and turned States witness. In 1980, Marino was convicted of second-degree murder and attempted murder but the case was overturned. He died of a heart attack in February of 1983. The San Jose/ San Diego Mob is virtually nonexistence today.

Sinatra in Havana: When the National syndicate held its conclave in Cuba in the 1940s, the Fischetti brothers were there with Frank Sinatra. (1915-1998) Sinatra later explained that he wasn't aware that the Fischetti's were gangsters and that he had first met them in Chicago during a benefit at the Chez Paree, a night club owned and managed by the Mob. The Fischetti's, Sinatra claimed, were star struck and insisted Sinatra use their cars and boats while he was in town and from that a friendship developed.

In early January of 1947, Rocca Fischetti called Sinatra and asked him to join him down in Havana. Sinatra agreed and on January 13 1947 Sinatra requested a gun permit, saying that he sometimes carried large sums of money and needed the gun for protection. Sinatra flew to New York and then to Miami where he stayed at Charlie Fischetti mansion. The night before leaving for Havana, Sinatra and Joe Fischetti were spotted in the Colonial Inn, the casino in Hallendale owned by Frank Costello (1891-1973) and New Jersey boss Joe Adonis (Born Joe Doto 1902-1972) and Meyer Lansky where Sinatra put on a free concert.

Charlie Fischetti (left facing camera) and his brother Rocco (right seated in chair)

On February 11, 1947, Sinatra and the Fischetti's were photographed walking down the steps of a Pan American clipper at the Havana airport. They checked into Meyer Lansky's Hotel, the Nacional, where 36 suites had been reserved for the Mob bosses which included Albert Anastasia, (1903-1957) Carlo Gambino, Willie Moretti, (1894-1951) Vito Genovese, (1897-1969) Frank Costello, Augie Pisano (? -1959) Joe Fat Man Magliocco, (1898-1963) Joe Bonanno, Tommy Three finger Brown Lucchese, (circa 1900-1967) Joe Profaci, Joe Adonis Tony Accardo, Sam Giancana, (1908-1975) Carlo Marcello, (1910-1993) Dandy Phil Kastel, Santo Trafficante and Meyer Lansky and Jospeh Doc Stacher who now controlled Lansky Juke boxes and slot machines in Jersey City.

Sinatra wasn't in the mob meeting, in Havana, but he was in the hotel. The singer had arrived in Havana, by plane, with the Fischetti brothers. Another story that made the rounds, then and now, and later portrayed in the film, The Godfather, was that Rocco Fischetti had several travel bags stuffed with two million dollars, the proceeds from narcotics sales that was owed to Lucky Luciano. (1897-1962) Terrified that he would be stopped and searched as he left the United States, Fischetti had brought Sinatra along to carry the bags into Cuba, were tailing him.

Traditionally, star struck customs agents didn't check celebrity's baggage.

Actually, a writer named Lee Mortimer (Born in Chicago as Mortimer Lieberman in 1906) spread the money in the suit case story. Mortimer disliked Sinatra intensely and at one time the dispute brought the two men to blows. The FBI added to Mortimor's story. Sinatra denied the story saying "if you can show me how to get two million dollars into a briefcase, I'll give you the two million dollars"

The fact is, the syndicate didn't need Frank Sinatra to lug around its dope proceeds for them. They had worked out a transportation system years ago thanks to the genius of Meyer Lansky. If they had to lug it across the country, as Sam Giancana said later "Sinatra is the last guy you would use for that. He would draw attention. When you transport money you always use a woman with a child or a grandmotherly type. Not movie stars"

Sica Gang: The Sica's were a group of brothers from New Jersey and led by eldest brother, Joseph, called JS, who held court in the famous Formosa Café. (7156 Santa Monica Blvd West Hollywood)

Freddie "Soft Freddie" Sica

The brothers worked closely with Mickey Cohen and the Chicago Outfit in busting up James Regan's Continental Race offices in Los Angeles. The brothers main contact with the national syndicate was through Jack Dragna, who was, unlike the Sica's, a made member of the Mafia. In turn, Dragna's main contact to the New York Families was Prize Fight impresario Frankie Carbo. The bulk of the Sica's criminal empire, which stretched from San Diego to San Jose, was the importation and distribution of heroin and control of gambling in the black neighborhoods of Los Angeles. The gang died off in the 1980s.

Stompanato, Johnny Jr. Born October 9, 1925 Died April 4, 1958. Stompanato, a former US Marine was one of drug dealer Mickey Cohen's main men around LA in the late 1950s.

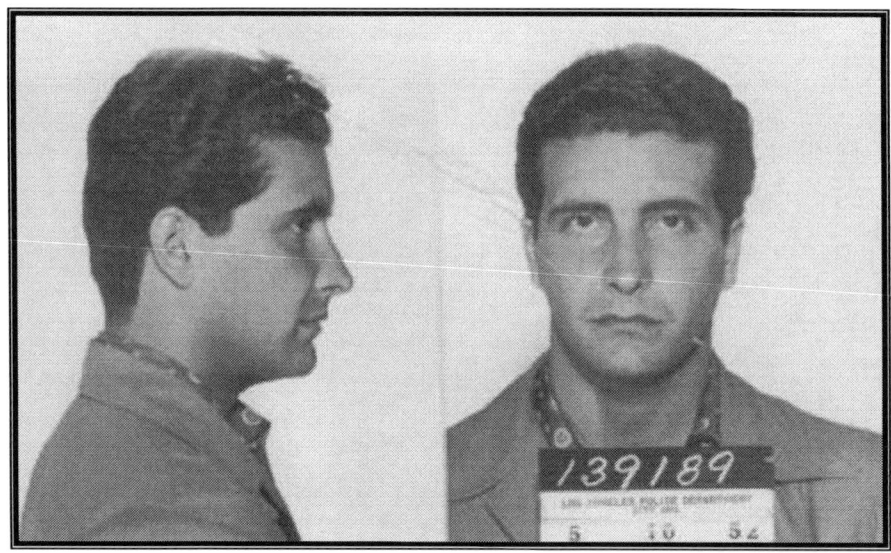

Stompanato

Stompanato came from a relatively stable middle class home in Woodstock Illinois. Unlike most people in his line of work, all considered, Stompanato was well educated and well-traveled.

Stompanato and his boss, Mickey Cohen and with Lana Turner (below)

After a stint as a marine in Asia, where he saw action, the gangster remained in China for several years working at a series of jobs including a short stint as a member of the US Department of State.

He returned to the states in the early 1950s, with a Turkish wife and an infant son, and made his way out to Hollywood.

By 1957, he was involved with the actress Lana Turner. Supposedly, while filming Another Time, Another Place, Turner was having an affair with her costar, actor Sean Connery.

Turner in Sunglasses, shows up for court

Stompanato allegedly rushed onto the set and threatened Connery, a former Mister World body building champion, disarmed the gangsters and tossed him off the set.

Stompanato dead

On April 4, 1958, Stompanato was stabbed to death at Turner's Beverly Hills home. Officially, the assailant was Turner's then teenage daughter, Cheryl, who claimed she stabbed the gangster to defend her mother from another of Stompanato's beatings.

Lana Turner, Stompanato and Cheryl Crane

The killing was ruled a justifiable homicide. Many doubt that Cheryl Crane actually stabbed Stompanato, believing instead that it was Turner who really killed the hoodlum.

Televised Mobsters: Television, and the image it presents of mobsters as the premier evil in America, has always been a thorn in the side of organized criminals.

The hoods' problems with television began when United States Senator Estes Kefauver introduced a resolution on January 5, 1950, calling for a sweeping examination of organized crime in America.

That in itself was nothing for the hoods to be worried about. For decades, some politician someplace was always calling for another investigation into organized crime. But this time it would be different, these hearings, the Kefauver hearings, would be televised for the entire country to see.

Senator Kefauver

The Kefauver Committee traveled 52,000 miles to fifteen cities to hold its

hearings while some 30 million Americans watched as the mobsters were grilled. By the time the committee ended in May of 1952, eighty-six percent of American homes were watching the hearings religiously.

Overnight millions of Americans knew the names Kefauver along with Jake Guzak, Charles Fischetti, Tony Accardo and others. The committee called more than 600 witnesses, compiled 11,500 pages of testimony.

Yet, not one of the 22 contempt of court cases stemming from the investigation held up in court. Of the 221 proposals submitted to Congress by the committee less than 10% were enacted into law. But, if the Kefauver committee accomplished nothing else, it dragged organized crime out of the shadows, the place where it operates the most effectively, and brought it out into the glare of television lights where the almighty hoods were, as writer William Brashler put it, "prodded and poked at by committee members like freshly captured rhinos."

Watching the hearings

While the committee may have failed as a practical lawmaking venture, it did propel Estes Kefauver out of obscurity. Aside from a spectacular bid for the Presidency in 1952, he became one of the best known and most widely respected men in America. He was in constant demand on the lecture circuit, earning as much as $25,000 for personal appearances. A book that was ghost-written in his name made the New York Times bestseller list for three months and CBS television placed him under contract to do the narration for a CBS show called "Crime Syndicated" and Hollywood beckoned him for the introductory narration for Humphrey Bogart's film "The Enforcer." Television producers and politicians, especially the Kennedy brothers, watched in wonder as Kefauver's career skyrocketed and realized there was a future in televised gangsters.

Elliot Ness

Hollywood saw the future in televised gangsters as well, and shortly after the Kefauver committee folded its tent, the TV waves were flooded with gangster epics, but none was as successful as "The Untouchables." Al Capone probably never knew Elliot Ness's name, since, for the Capone organization, Ness and his group of so-called "Untouchables," government agents who were supposed to be unbribable were a mere nuisance more than anything else. Elliot Ness died in 1957, his exploits against Capone almost unknown and forgotten. However, a few days before his death, Ness's biography "The Untouchables" was published. The book, complete with occasional embellishments, sold well and Hollywood, specifically Desi-Lu productions, which was owned by Desi Arnez and Luci Ball, decided that Ness's exploits, properly rewritten, would make a fine television show.

The Untouchables

They were right. In its first season, The Untouchables, starring John Kennedy's former roommate Robert Stack, was a smash hit. It was also an odd twist of fate that the comedian Gary Morton, who would eventually marry Luci Ball, had once been married to Judy Campbell's sister Jackie. But, the show didn't go over well with the Mafia, which still operated, more or less, as an unknown entity. What's more, the mob in 1960 was ruled over by men who had known Capone and Nitti and were fond of them.

Gary Morton and Ball

The national commission figured, correctly, that by allowing the show to air that it would set a precedent. After all, they reasoned, if the outfit were allowed to be discussed openly on television, what was next? "So the council had a meet about it," wrote Lucky Luciano, "and one of the guys in Profaci's outfit named Joe Colombo come up with the idea of forming a legitimate association of Americans with Italian backgrounds to start a campaign against usin' just Italian names for them gangsters in the TV shows and movies. The whole idea was to try and get The Untouchables off the fuckin' air."

Joe Profaci

Joe Colombo

The syndicate backed Colombo's idea and put money into something called the Federation of Italian American Democratic Organizations, headed by US Congressman Alfred Santangelo, who, according to Luciano, knew from the start that the entire organization was dreamed up and manufactured by the mob.

Santangelo

The federation launched a boycott against the program's sponsor, Ligget & Myers Tobacco Company, who eventually withdrew their support from the show.   But the boycott that was supposed to take the show off the air had just the opposite effect. When word of the Mafia-backed ban made the press, the show's rating went through the roof and Chesterfield cigarettes was back as the program's sponsor.

Exasperated, the Chicago mob's elders put Johnny Roselli, their west coast representative, on the case. Roselli recruited L.A mobster Jimmy "The Weasel" Fratianno to fix the problem by shooting Desi Arnez, the show's primary producer.

Jimmy the Weasel

"Millions of people all over the world see this show every fucking week," Roselli told Fratianno. "It's even popular in Italy. And what they see is a bunch of Italian lunatics running around with machine guns, talking out of the corner of their mouths, slopping spaghetti like a bunch of fucking pigs. They make Capone and Nitti look like bloodthirsty maniacs. The top guys have voted a hit. We're going to clip Desi Arnez the producer of the show." Eventually, cooler heads prevailed and it was decided that killing Arnez, who was one of the world's most popular entertainment personalities, would only cause more problems than it would solve, but, still, the boys still wanted the show taken off the air.

Desi Arnez

Since Arnez was leasing space to Frank Sinatra's production company at Desilu studios, where Arnez was also filming The Untouchables, Tony Accardo told Sam Giancana to contact Frank Sinatra and have him talk some sense into Arnez. While a direct order from the Godfather himself would have scared most Americans, for a wanna-be gangster like Sinatra, it was almost an orgasmic experience.

Provine

In late April of 1961, Sinatra, actress Dorothy Provine and Jimmy Van Heusen drove to the Indian Wells Country Club and waited in the restaurant, where Arnez ended most evenings at the bar, when Arnez walked in flanked by two massive bodyguards.

Jimmy Van Heusen

Almost on schedule, Arnez strolled into the club, dwarfed by his bodyguards. Spotting Sinatra, Arnez yelled across the room, "Hi Ya Dago!" and then walked over to Sinatra's table.

Sinatra was all business and got right to the point. He told Arnez that his Italian gangster friends didn't like the Untouchable program and that it made all Italians look like killers. Arnez, slurred with whiskey, replied: "What do you want me to do Frank, make them all Jews?" Except in his thick Cuban accent it came out "U's."

"You want them all to be U's, Frankie? Huh? Let me tell you something, I remember you when jew couldn't get a yob Frankie, couldn't get a yob! So why don't you forget all this bullshit and just have your drinks and enjoy yourself? Stop getting your nose in where it doesn't belong you and your so-called friends," and then walked away leaving a castrated Sinatra to say "I couldn't hit him, we've been friends for too long." At around 4:00 A.M. Sinatra's group, boozed up, left the bar and went to Van Heusen's house in Palm Desert, with Sinatra still fuming over the humiliation he had taken from Arnez.

Once inside Van Heusen's house, Sinatra exploded and attacked an original painting by Norman Rockwell, carving it up with a kitchen knife. "If you try to fix that or put it back," he told Van Heusen, "I will come and blow the fucking house up."

The Untouchables not only stayed on the air, it became a classic and spawned a film and started television's love affair with gangsters. When Bobby Kennedy decided to turn on the mob, the most effective move he made against them was to focus attention on it, by calling press conferences to discuss the Justice Department's progress against the outfit, by referring to the Dons by their full names.

That was bad enough, until finally, to the mob's horror, Kennedy damaged them the most by putting a made member of the New York Mafia, a hood named Joe Valachi, on nationwide television to tell what he knew about the mob in America. The Bureau of Narcotics had nailed Valachi and had him put away in a Federal Prison in Atlanta for fifteen years on a dope peddling charge.

Joe Valachi

Normally, a career hood like Valachi would have done time and suffered quietly, but Valachi heard that the mob suspected him of being an informant and intended to kill him as he walked through the prison yard. Understandably paranoid, Valachi mistook an otherwise innocent con for a mob assassin and cracked open his skull with an iron bar, killing him instantly.

Now facing a murder rap and with mob killers still lurking in the shadows, Valachi set a precedent for hundreds of other mobsters; he turned informant. Valachi's flip and the justification this would give to the Department of Justice was so important that Robert Kennedy flew down to Atlanta to interview the gangster himself. Valachi later told the FBI that Kennedy had promised him freedom and a new life if he cooperated and testified before Congress. When it looked like Kennedy intended to renege on the deal, Valachi set fire to his jail cell in protest. When the matter was reported to Attorney General Kennedy he said, "Tell Valachi to knock it off...or we'll set him free."

Ethel Kennedy, wife of then Attorney General Robert F. Kennedy was present at the Valachi testimony

Valachi's riveting testimony before Congress, covered live on national television, confirmed that there was a national crime syndicate in operation in every major city in the country. Furthermore, Valachi named 289-suspected Mob members and outlined the five major mob families and their inner workings. Most of the testimony Valachi gave to Congress was unusable in court for one reason or another, but that didn't matter.

Valachi had served his purpose because what Robert Kennedy wanted the most out of Valachi's testimony was to shake up Congress. After Valachi appeared before the House, Congress passed a series of laws, suggested by RFK, that would allow legal wiretapping on a massive scale and for the Justice Department to be able to offer immunity to witnesses against the mob. Valachi's last words to Congress before he stepped down from his testimony, were prophetic. Perhaps referring to John Kennedy, the gangster looked slowly across the members of the panel and said, "Gentlemen, I'll say this. Someday the mob is going to put a man in the White House, and he's not going to know it until they present him with the bill."

In their own words

"I never killed a guy who didn't deserve it." **Mickey Cohen.**

"I got a kick out of having a big bankroll in my pocket. Even if I only made a couple hundred dollars, I'd always keep it in fives and tens so it'd look big."
Mickey Cohen.

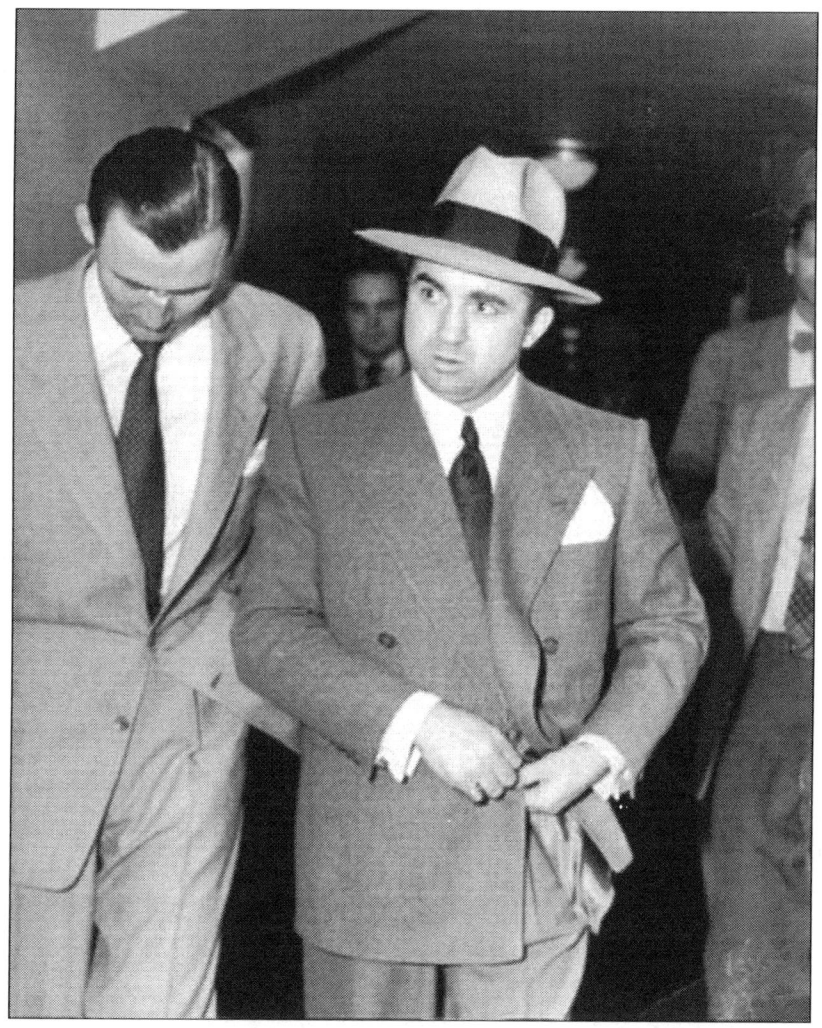

"I started rooting - you know, sticking up joints - with some older guys. By now I had gotten a taste of what the racket world really was - the glamour, the way they dressed, the way they always had a pocketful of money." **Mickey Cohen.**

"It's the first time in my life I've ever seen a dead man convicted of his own murder. So far as that jury's concerned, Johnny just walked too close to that knife." **Mickey Cohen on the death of his driver Johnny Stompanato**

'Let's show 'em. 'Let's show those asshole Hollywood fruitcakes that they can't get away with it as if nothing's happened. Let's hit Sinatra. Or I could whack out a couple of those other guys, (Peter) Lawford and that (Dean) Martin, and I could take the nigger (Sammy Davis) and put his other eye out.' **Mafia associate to Sam Giancana in a recorded phone conversation in 1963. Giancana's response was. 'Nah, 'I've got other plans for them.'**

The other plans turned out to be "The Night of the Stars" An annual bash sponsored by the Italian Welfare Council, a real charity created up by Giancana and his wife. The concert was held at the Villa Venice Mobsters sold tickets to the event which featured Bob Hope, Dean Martin, Jerry Lewis Jimmy Durante, and Frank Sinatra. Very little of the money actual made it to poor Italians. Using shrewd accountants, Giancana managed to pocket most of the cash through dummy companies who billed the events for services at twice the usual rate.

Made in the USA
San Bernardino, CA
30 May 2016